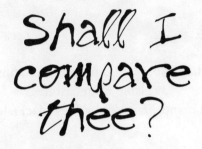

Other books of humorous quotations
available from Prion:
Wit and *More Wit* by Des MacHale

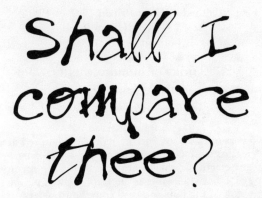

Shall I compare thee?

A witty collection of quotable similes

ROSEMARIE JARSKI

PRION

First published in Great Britain 1997 by PRION
32-34 Gordon House Road,
London NW5 1LP

Copyright © Rosemarie Jarski 1997

A catalogue record of this book can be obtained
from the British Library

ISBN 1-85375-259-2

Printed and bound in Great Britain by
Creative Print and Design, Wales

Contents

Introduction

THERE was a story in *The Times* a while back, about a Professor of English at the University of New Hampshire named Donald Silva. During a lecture, Professor Silva attempted to illustrate the concept of a simile by likening belly dancing to 'a jelly on a plate, with a vibrator under the plate.' A group of female students complained and a university court found him guilty of 'verbal sexual harassment'. He was suspended for a year without pay.

Such is the might of a simile. Its power to conjure up a vivid visual image can inflame the imagination, stir up emotion, ignite passion, provoke outrage, and even get you fired.

The similes in this book may do some or all of those things but, above all, they aim to make you do the one thing that the group of female students at the University of New Hampshire failed to do: smile.

A simile is perfectly shaped to tickle the funny bone (for those of us that have one). The sudden recognition of a resemblance between two unrelated images delights in much the same way as wit.

And the colourful imagery means a simile sticks in the memory. Once Colette tells us the crescent-moon looks like a fingernail-cutting, it's hard to see it any other way.

From Colette to Noel Coward, the similes have been gathered from numerous sources, some more fertile than others. Trying to find a simile in the works of Jane Austen is like trying to find a strand of straw in a gigantic stack of needles. The one I did find probably belongs in the British Museum, under glass.

Contrast P.G. Wodehouse who dazzles us with similes on nearly every page, each one a diamond of wit and originality. Raymond Chandler's similes are as plentiful, if more hard-boiled. Smart-ass, streetwise, they wear their collars up high, their hats down low, and shoot from the hip in a voice that's pure Bogie. Soft-centred and irresistibly silly, the similes of *Blackadder* are as integral to the shows as Baldric's 'cunning plans'– and a lot more successful.

Like a public-toilet, you can never find a simile when you really need one. 'My love is like a red, red ...er ... er ... uhm ...' See under: Love. Arranged by theme, the similes are quick and easy to locate – for instant light relief.

Purists will quibble that some comparisons included aren't 'proper' similes. Yes, but 'improper' similes can fun too, and this collection makes no distinction where that's involved.

The aim is to provide amusement. Service with a simile. As proof of success, I eagerly await complaint from a certain group of female students at the University of New Hampshire.

Footnote: Professor Silva successfully counter-sued to overturn his suspension and received compensation from the university for his humiliation. We can only hope his unfortunate experience has not inhibited his obvious flair for similes.

Appearance

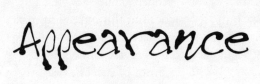

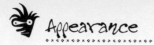

General

He looked rather pleasantly like a blond
Satan.

Dashiel Hammett

She looked more like Marilyn Monroe than
anything human.

P.G. Wodehouse

A bit like Elizabeth Taylor, but definitely a
bowdlerized version.

William McIlvanney, *Remedy is None*

The old Italian making sandwiches looked
just like Rudolph Valentino if Rudolph
Valentino had been an old Italian making
sandwiches.

Richard Brautigan, *Dreaming of Babylon*

She looked a lot like Hitler except for the moustache – hers was bigger.

Anon.

Pandora said I looked like Noel Coward in my new bri-nylon dressing gown. I said, 'Thanks, Pandora', although to be honest I don't know who Noel Coward is or was. I hope he's not a mass murderer or anything.

Sue Townsend, *The Secret Diary of Adrian Mole aged 13³/4*

He looked like an accountant or serial killer-type. Definitely one of the service industries.

Kinky Friedman, *Elvis, Jesus and Coca-Cola*

Even librarians who try not to look like librarians look like librarians trying not to look like librarians.

Anon.

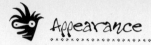
Appearance

'The gentleman who came to the flat wears horn-rimmed spectacles, sir.'
'And looked like something on a slab?'
'Possibly there is a certain suggestion of the piscine, sir.'
'Then it must be Gussie.'

P.G. Wodehouse, *Stiff Upper Lip, Jeeves*

She had rouged her cheeks to a colour otherwise seen only on specially ordered Pontiac Firebirds.

George V. Higgins, *Wall Street Journal*

She had the rough, blowsy and somewhat old-fashioned look of a whore of the Renoir period.

Thomas Wolfe

Like successful nuns, she had a slightly married air.

Elizabeth Bowen

Well, don't stand there, Miss Preen. You look like frozen custard.

Monty Wooley in *The Man Who Came to Dinner*, 1941

She always looks like she's been out in the rain feeding the poultry.

Clifton Webb in *The Dark Corner*, 1946

Now must I look as sober and demure as a whore at a christening.

George Farquhar

He looked as if he had just returned from spending an uncomfortable night in a very dark cave.

Edith Sitwell

You're welcome to take a bath. You look like the second week of the garbage strike.

Neil Simon, *The Gingerbread Lady*

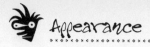

Ratso looked like an extra from the cast of
the movie *Coma*.

> Kinky Friedman, *When the Cat's Away*

She is a stern woman who looks as if her
idea of a good time would be knitting,
preferably under the guillotine.

> William McIlvanney, *The Kiln*

He looked like a horse with a secret sorrow.

> P.G. Wodehouse

A thoroughly insipid woman who reminds
one instantly of some of the hairier urchins.

> Woody Allen

She had skin like a reptile.

> James Caan in *Honeymoon in Vegas*, 1992

He looked like a horse who, in addition to
having a secret sorrow, had laryngitis as well.

> P.G. Wodehouse

All I say is, nobody has any business to go around looking like a horse and behaving as if it were all right. You don't catch horses going around looking like people do you?

Dorothy Parker, *Horsie*

A passport picture is a photo of a man that he can laugh at without realising that it looks exactly the way his friends see him.

The Boston Herald

The diabolical old man reminded Nately of his father because the two were nothing at all alike.

Joseph Heller, *Catch-22*

He's built like a Coke machine.

Joseph Wambaugh

His neck looked as if it could dent an ax.

Richard Brautigan, *Dreaming of Babylon*

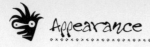 Appearance

He looks as if he's been caught with his
pants down at a nuns' picnic.

Richard Brautigan, *Dreaming of Babylon*

'What you got there?'
'What's it look like?'
'A penis, only smaller.'

Bernadette Peters in *Pink Cadillac*, 1989

The myth of all penises being equal...started,
I can only conclude, by a sexologist who had
the misfortune to be hung like a hamster.

Julie Burchill, *Arena* magazine

You know Linford Christie ... my genitals
are like a sort of travel version of that.

Frank Skinner

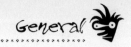

Are you eating a tomato or is that your
nose?

W.C. Fields in *You Can't Cheat an Honest Man*, 1939

His nose peels in August like a jersey potato.

Craig Raine, *Misericords*

There were memories of Africa in him, like
the great event of the nose, which resembled
the back of a black bullfrog squatting on his
face.

Martin Amis, *The Information*

He had a pair of buckteeth that made him
look like the first cousin of a walrus.

Richard Brautigan, *Dreaming of Babylon*

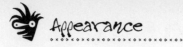
Appearance

Your toes are like tombstones.

Alain Delon to Marianne Faithfull in *Girl on a Motorcyle*, 1968

Beauty & Ugliness

My dear, you look like Helen of Troy after a good facial!

P.G. Wodehouse, *Uncle Dynamite*

All women are beautiful, like a toilet bowl, when you need one.

John Updike, *Couples*

Beautiful as a blank cheque.

Clive James

Beautiful as a rich orphan.

Gelett Burgess

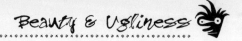

She was so beautiful that the advertising people would have made her into a national park if they would have gotten their hands on her.

Richard Brautigan, *Revenge of the Lawn*

Artie, she's a nice girl, but it's like sitting in a room with a beautiful vase.

Judy Garland on Lana Turner

Lord Illingworth told me this morning that there was an orchid in the conservatory as beautiful as the seven deadly sins.

Oscar Wilde

Hell hath no vanity like a handsome man.

Coco Chanel

Handsome as a hernia.

Gene Weingarten, *The Washington Post*

Appearance

I was so handsome that women became spellbound when I came into view. In San Francisco, in rainy seasons, I was frequently mistaken for a cloudless day.

Mark Twain

Shall I compare thee to a summer's day? Thou art more lovely and more temperate.

William Shakespeare

The problem with beauty is that it's like being born rich and getting progressively poorer.

Joan Collins

Sidney, was I hit by a bus? I look as though I were hit by a fully-loaded, guided-tour bus.

Maggie Smith in *California Suite*, 1989

She was always wearing a loose bathrobe that covered up a body that would have won first prize in a beauty contest for cement blocks.

Richard Brautigan, *Dreaming of Babylon*

He looked like the victim of a forceps delivery.

Auberon Waugh, *Private Eye*

He was as ugly as a gargoyle hewn by a drunken stonesman for the adornment of a Methodist Chapel in one of the vilest suburbs of Leeds or Wigan.

Max Beerbohm

Face

She was a really bad-looking girl. Facially she resembled Louis Armstrong's voice.

Woody Allen

He had a face like a collapsed lung.

Raymond Chandler, *The Long Goodbye*

A face so elaborately pock-marked that all he'd have to do is suck an American flag and he'd be the spit of the surface of the moon.

David Baddiel, *Time For Bed*

Her face looked like something on the menu in a seafood restaurant.

Woody Allen

Descriptions of my face have included comparisons with most root vegetables.

Frankie Howerd

A face like Walt Disney's idea of a grandfather.

William McIlvanney, *Laidlaw*

His flat face looked as if it were pressed against a window, except there was no window.

Rebecca West

Looks

He looked at me as if I was a side dish he hadn't ordered.

Ring Lardner

She gave me the sort of look she would have given a leper she wasn't fond of.

P.G. Wodehouse, *Ice in the Bedroom*

One of those sidelong looks that women think men don't understand, the kind that feel like a dentist's drill

Raymond Chandler, *Mandarin's Jade*

We looked at each other with the clear innocent eyes of a couple of used-car salesmen.

Raymond Chandler, *The High Window*

He stared with the intensity of a man having a private audience with an angel.

James Morrow

'Dance?'
She looks at you as if you had just suggested instrumental rape.

Jay McInerney, *Bright Lights, Big City*

Eyes

His eyes look like a left-luggage office.

A.A. Gill, *The Sunday Times*

Her eyes burst open – whoosh! like blue umbrellas.

Angela Carter, *Nights at the Circus*

She's got those eyes that run up and down men like a searchlight.

Dennie Moore in *The Women*, 1939

Large dark eyes that looked as if they might warm up at the right time and in the right place.

Raymond Chandler, *The Lady in the Lake*

They are the sort of eyes the passionless would describe as come-to-bed eyes. They aren't come-to-bed eyes. Who needs a bed?

William McIlvanney, *The Kiln*

When she raises her eyelids it's as if she were taking off all her clothes.

Colette

'You have beautiful eyes.'
'They're nothing compared to my tits.'

Kevin Kline and Teri Hatcher in *Soapdish*, 1991

Breasts

How do you like them? Like a pear, a lemon, à la Montgolfier, half an apple, or a cantaloup? Go on, choose, don't be embarrassed.

Colette

Breasts are like the pillows of all sweet dreams.

Langston Hughes, *Midnight Dancer*

Piercing boobs heaving in a frock closely resembling a two-car garage.

Clive James

She thrust out her meagre bosom as if to let a caged bird within it free.

Angela Carter, *Nights at the Circus*

Her breasts filled out the front of her blouse like the humps of a small camel. Not the kind you smoke, but the kind you ride.

Kinky Friedman, *When the Cat's Away*

I could feel her nipples boring into my chest. They were harder than Japanese arithmetic.

Kinky Friedman, *Frequent Flyer*

He twisted my nipples as though tuning a radio.

Lisa Alther, *Kinflicks*

She had such big tits, she looked like her arm was in a sling.

Alan Bennett

When she laughed, her chest heaved; it was
like watching those bouncy balls in a Disney
singalong tape.

Max Rose

Jogging, bra-less, by the canal, she looked
like the original inspiration for Barnes Wallis.

Ann Winter

Breasts came back after World War II …
linked with dumb blondes in the most
regrettable partnership since the sweet potato
met the marshmallow.

Laura Shapiro, *Newsweek*

Did you see the Baywatch Babes make an
entrance? It was like silicone valley in earth-
quake season·

Ben Elton, *Popcorn*

Kim Basinger lies on her back naked, her
bosom pointing straight up like two rocks of
Gibraltar topped by cruise missiles ready to
blow the roof off.

Mark Steyn, *The Spectator*

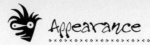

Appearance

Demi Moore's breasts hang around *Striptease*
like a brace of silicon albatrosses.

Mark Steyn, The Spectator

Elizabeth Taylor looks like two small boys
fighting underneath a mink blanket.

Blackwell

Working with Sophia Loren is like being
bombed with water melons.

Alan Ladd

The push-up bra was the equivalent to me
of Einstein's theory of relativity.

Dolly Parton

In a sweater she looked like a walking dairy
State.

Joan Rivers

Implants are about as natural as Pop Tarts.

Lowri Turner

A cleavage which looks as if it should be
offering day trips.

Jaci Stephen

Walk

You walked in to the party,
Like you were walking onto a yacht.

Carly Simon, 'You're so Vain'

Look how she moves. That's just like Jell-O
with springs.

Jack Lemmon on Marilyn Monroe in *Some Like it Hot*, 1959

She walked across the ballroom as if she
were trudging through deep snow.

Noel Coward

The guys walked very business-like, as if they
were characters in a Warner Brothers gangster
movie.

Richard Brautigan, *Dreaming of Babylon*

Walking in Hollywood is tantamount to
loitering with intent.

Anon.

He walked as if he had fouled his
small-clothes and smelt it.

Christopher Smart

As foolish as it must seem to the crab when
he sees man walking forwards.

Georg Christoph Lichtenberg

His footsteps echoed away like a woodpecker
falling asleep.

Boris Vian

Dance

Dancing with her was like moving a piano.

Ring W. Lardner

He danced like a man with a poor personality.

Simon Nye, *Wideboy*

Have you seen him dance? Like God, he moves in mysterious ways.

Ann Winter

He intensified the silent passion of his dancing, trying to convey the impression of being something South American, which ought to be chained up and muzzled in the interests of pure womanhood.

P.G. Wodehouse, *Nothing Serious*

He dances like a drunk killing cockroaches.

John Barbour

She does a dance suggesting the life of a fern; I saw one of the rehearsals, and to me it would have equally well suggested the life of John Wesley.

Saki

You would get something of the same thrill if 16 people were to brush their teeth in perfect unison to the beat of a jaunty reel.

Thomas Sutcliffe on *Riverdance* on TV, *The Independent*

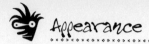

Hair

Why don't you get a haircut? You look like a chrysanthemum.

P.G. Wodehouse

I mean for my hair to look like this.

Ellen DeGeneres, *My Point...And I do have one*

A lady whose upswept hairstyle ... suggested that she had surfaced abruptly underneath a heron's nest.

Clive James

Her hair was rich as a wild bee's nest and her eyes were full of stings.

Laurie Lee, *Cider With Rosie*

I suppose if Ginny stays she'll grow up to look like that: blonde hair, blonde teeth, blonde life.

Jane Fonda in *California Suite*, 1989

Blondes are the best victims. They're like virgin snow which shows up the bloody foot-
prints.

Alfred Hitchcock

As blonde as a Zulu under the bleach and as
to disposition as soft as a sidewalk.

Raymond Chandler, *The Long Goodbye*

Her hair lounges on her shoulders like an
anaesthetized cocker spaniel.

Henry Allen, *The Washington Post*

A few locks of dry white hair clung to his
scalp like wild flowers fighting for life on a
bare rock.

Raymond Chandler, *The Big Sleep*

He wore baldness like an expensive hat.

Gloria Swanson on Cecil B. de Mille

Jinty Adamson lived high up in a grey block
of flats, as accessible as a bald Rapunzel.

William McIlvanney, *The Papers of Tony Veitch*

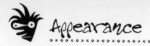 Appearance

Hair like badly turned broccoli.

> Clive James on John McEnroe

He says my moustache is like the faint discoloured smear left by a squashed black-beetle on the side of a kitchen sink.

> P.G. Wodehouse, *The Code of the Woosters*

He looks like an explosion in a pubic hair factory.

> Jonathan Miller on Paul Johnson

My pubic hair is a problem ... it's all over the place, like some bloody rockery plant.

> Victoria Wood

Underarm hair ... dark and thick, like exotic underbush from the Brazilian rain forest, the extract of which might cure cancer.

> Laramie Dunaway, *Women on Top*

His shirt was open at the neck, and he had such a hairy chest he looked like a burst sofa.

Les Dawson

He may have hair upon his chest But sister, so has Lassie ...

Cole Porter, *I Hate Men*

Smile

A smile like a dirty-minded cherub.

Anon. on Christopher Isherwood

A smile like the silver plate on a coffin.

John Philpot Curran on Robert Peel

His smile bathed us like warm custard.

Basil Boothroyd

She gave him a lovely smile and he looked as if he had shaken hands with God.

Raymond Chandler, *The Long Goodbye*

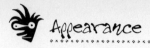

He had a smile on his face but it was about
as thin as airline coffee.

> Kinky Friedman, *When the Cat's Away*

I just smiled serenely like a Moonie on LSD.

> Kinky Friedman, *Greenwich Killing Time*

The smile disappeared quicker than a rain
forest.

> Kinky Friedman, *Musical Chairs*

Laugh

Like an old Chevrolet starting up on a
below-freezing morning.

> Anon. on Phyllis Diller

A laugh like a squadron of cavalry charging
over a tin bridge.

> P.G. Wodehouse, *Carry on, Jeeves*

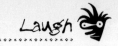

A high, musical, merry laugh, like the singing of field mice going forth to gather grain in a land where the hawks are all vegetarians.

Tom Robbins, *Skinny Legs and All*

A laugh as jolly as an axe embedding itself in a skull.

William McIlvanney, *The Kiln*

Her laughter sounded so canned you could almost taste the botulism breeding in it.

Kinky Friedman, *Greenwich Killing Time*

She was giving the impression of a hyena which had just heard a good one from another hyena.

P.G. Wodehouse, *Much Obliged, Jeeves*

Her laughter hung in the air like sleigh bells on a winter night.

Jay Parini, *The Patch Boys*

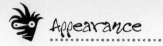

Voice

If a swamp alligator could talk, it would sound like Tennessee Williams.

> Rex Reed

His voice was sharp as a snowflake on a sun-burned nose.

> Rex Reed

My voice sounds like a mafioso pallbearer.

> Sylvester Stallone

The speaking voice sounds like Rice Krispies if they could talk.

> John Simon on Barbra Streisand

Ruby Wax talks like a cement mixer from Brooklyn.

> David Naughton

Voice

Talk as though you have a cathedral in your mouth.

> Peter Ustinov on how to imitate Harold Macmillan

I cannot bring myself to vote for a woman who has been voice-trained to speak to me as though my dog has just died.

> Keith Waterhouse on Margaret Thatcher

She sounded like the book of Revelations read out over a railway station public address system by a headmistress of a certain age wearing calico knickers.

> Clive James on Margaret Thatcher

She had a voice that made Pearl Harbor seem like a lullaby.

> Richard Brautigan, *Dreaming of Babylon*

His voice was intimate as the rustle of sheets.

> Dorothy Parker, *Dusk Before Fireworks*

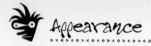

Appearance

A voice like the stuff they use to line summer clouds with.

Raymond Chandler, The Long Goodbye

A voice like ground-up heaven sieved through silk underwear.

Pete Stanton, Loaded magazine

A voice that reminded one of a fat bishop blessing a butter-making competition.

Saki

He could say the word 'succulent' in such a way that when you heard it you thought you were biting into a ripe peach.

Georg Christoph Lichtenberg

I knew a Jew fish crier down on Maxwell Street with a voice like a north wind blowing over corn stubble in January.

Carl Sandburg

Voice

◇‹◊›‹◊›‹◊›‹◊›‹◊›‹◊›‹◊›‹◊›‹◊›‹◊›‹◊›‹◊›‹◊›‹◊›‹◊›‹◊›‹◊›‹◊›

He was a guy who talked with commas, like
a heavy novel.

> Raymond Chandler, *The Long Goodbye*

Miss Harthill's voice is quintessentially Radio
4, like someone talking down a would-be
suicide from a high window-ledge.

> *The Listener*

That voice! She sounds as if she thinks a
crèche is something that happens on the M1.

> Jeananne Crowley

A voice like water going out of the bath.

> Geoffrey Madan

His voice faded off into a sort of sad whisper,
like a mortician asking for a down payment.

> Raymond Chandler, *The Little Sister*

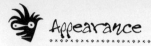

Smell

You smell like the toasted cheese sandwiches
my mother used to bring me.

Anthony Perkins in *Psycho II*, 1983

She smelled the way the Taj Mahal looks by
moonlight.

Raymond Chandler, *The Little Sister*

You smell good, like a bitch in a hothouse.

John Cusack in *The Grifters*, 1990

He smelled as if he had just eaten a mustard-
coated camel.

Martin Amis, *London Fields*

The elevator had an elderly perfume in it,
like three widows drinking tea.

Raymond Chandler, *The Big Sleep*

The place smelt of apple-scented air freshener, not like apples, but like a committee's idea of what apples smell like.

Joseph O'Connor, *Cowboys and Indians*

How could I know that murder sometimes smells like honeysuckle?

Fred MacMurray in *Double Indemnity*, 1944

I love the smell of napalm in the morning. It smells like victory.

Robert Duvall in *Apocalypse Now*, 1979

Clothes

My closet looks like a convention of multiple personality cases.

Anna Quindlen, *Newsmakers '93*

Marcia was incredibly organised. She folded her underwear like origami.

Linda Barnes

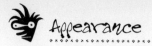

Jeeves lugged my purple socks out of the drawer as if he were a vegetarian fishing a caterpillar out of his salad.

P.G. Wodehouse, *My Man Jeeves*

All right, girls ... get into the cable-knit mohair sweaters, the ones that fluff out like a cat by a project heating duct.

Tom Wolfe, *The Kandy-Kolored Tangerine-Flake Streamline Baby*

A blonde in jeans so tight her hipbones looked like towel hooks.

Erma Bombeck

If that dress had pockets, you'd look like a pool table.

Rodney Dangerfield in *Back to School* 1986

I don't own a dress. I wear skirts but I look like a netball teacher.

Victoria Wood

The skirt looks as if a horse had left her its second-best blanket.

Randall Jarrell, *Pictures From an Institution*

Men who wear turtlenecks look like turtles.

Doris Lilly, *The New York Post*

Her petticoat had stripes of broad red and blue and looked as though it had been made out of a stage-curtain. I would have paid a lot for a front seat, but there was no performance.

Georg Christoph Lichtenberg

I've blown the rent on suits that make me look like an Italian Lambretta dealer.

A.A. Gill, *The Sunday Times*

That suit fits like a glove ... it sticks out in five places.

Dame Edna Everage

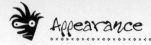

Compared with him, an audience of AC/DC heavy-metal fans would win prizes for couture.

The Observer on the dress-sense of designer, Alexander McQueen, head of the House of Givenchy

Some people are born with a sense of how to clothe themselves, others acquire it, others look as if their clothes had been thrust upon them

Saki

In his labial-pink jacket with his mouth agape, he looked like a large, disbelieving codfish.

Kinky Friedman, *Frequent Flyer*

Frank's white shirts usually looked like they had been rinsed out in a bucket of cold coffee.

Simon Nye, *Wideboy*

A shirt that looked like it had once belonged to Engelbert Humperdinck.

Kinky Friedman, *God Bless John Wayne*

His clothes looked as if they had been brought up by someone else.

Dorothy Parker

Where's the man could ease a heart like a satin gown?

Dorothy Parker, *Dusk Before Fireworks*

Such garments as hers did not just occur; like great poetry, they required labour.

Dorothy Parker, *The Custard Heart*

English women's shoes look as if they had been made by someone who had often heard shoes described but had never seen any.

Margaret Halsey

Garbo's feet were beautiful and long ... but she had an unfortunate habit of encasing them in huge brown 'loafers' which gave the impression that she wore landing craft.

David Niven

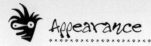 Appearance

I am still looking for a pair of training shoes that will make running on streets seem like running barefoot across the bosoms of maidens.

Dave Brosnan

The Body

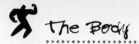

Health

I cannot keep myself healthy – too many bad
habits deeply ingrained, cardiac bronchitis
like the orchestra of death tuning up under
water.

Anthony Burgess

Oh! When I have the gout, I feel as if I am
walking on my eyeballs.

Sydney Smith

He's running a high temperature and his
chest looks like a bad Matisse.

Noel Coward on a man with chicken pox

Our bowels were like running faucets.

John Farris, *Wildwood*

Her manner of enquiring after a trifling ailment gave one the impression that she was more concerned with the fortunes of the malady than with oneself, and when one got rid of a cold one felt that she almost expected to be given its postal address.

Saki

The doctor carried his little black bag like a small sample cut from the shadow of death.

Helen Hudson, *Meyer, Meyer*

It's like a convent, the hospital. You leave the world behind and take vows of poverty, chastity, obedience.

Carole Wheat, *Life, for Short*

I had never seen Sister close to before. This unexpected proximity had the effect of being in a rowing-boat under the bows of the *Queen Mary*.

Richard Gordon, *Doctor in the House*

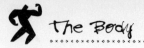

The appendix resembles a four-inch worm,
and like the Aldwych Tube leads nowhere.

Richard Gordon, Punch

A heart transplant operation is as simple as
changing the wheel on your car.

Richard Gordon, Punch

Griff: A Barium Meal goes in like liquid clay
and comes out like a sixty-two piece earthen-
ware tea-set.
Mel: What if you're constipated?
Griff: Well, then you've got an early Henry
Moore on your hands.

Smith and Jones

A woman went to a plastic surgeon and
asked him to make her like Bo Derek. He
gave her a lobotomy.

Joan Rivers

I need a valium the size of a hockey puck.

Woody Allen, Broadway Danny Rose, 1984

Psychiatry is like pool cleaning. In both professions you skim the surface, explore the murky depths, and add chemicals when necessary.

Frasier, US Sitcom

Diet & Fitness

As large as life and in fact twenty pounds larger.

Damon Runyon

He looks, at certain angles, like a cheeseburger with all the ingredients oozing awkwardly out of the bun.

Rex Reed

A 20-stone woman with buckling ankles smelt as if something had died in her creases.

A.A. Gill, *The Sunday Times*

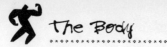

Are there advantages and disadvantages to being built like a planet?

Woody Allen

His wife had a gigantic rear end ... It looked like she was shoplifting throw pillows.

Frasier, US sitcom

Her great buttocks rolled like the swell on a heavy winter sea.

Miles Gibson, *Dancing With Mermaids*

What would cellulite actually look like? One thinks of wallpaper paste somehow.
Wallpaper the bathroom ceiling with your own cellulite.

Sue Limb, Dulcie Domum, *The Guardian*

I want to get as thin as my first husband's promises.

Texas Guinan

Liquid diets: the powder is mixed with water and tastes exactly like powder mixed with water.

Art Buchwald

Those magazine dieting stories always have the testimonial of a woman who wears a dress that could slipcover New Jersey in one photo and thirty days later looks like a well-dressed thermometer.

Erma Bombeck

After *One Flew Over the Cuckoo's Nest*, people think the psychiatric ward is where an evil and sadistic person humiliates depressed people which is actually a far more accurate description of Weight Watchers.

Jo Brand

The joggers looked like an organized death march as they ran by gasping, perspiring, stumbling, their faces contorted with pain.

Erma Bombeck

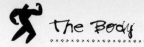

The Body

He runs five miles a day and has a body like Jean Claude Van Damme. Shame he still has a face like Gérard Depardieu.

Isabel Vale

Exercise is like a cold bath. You think it does you good because you feel better when you stop it.

Robert Quillen

Sports

Boxing

It's like any other business, only here the blood shows.

Kirk Douglas in *Champion*, 1949

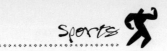

Wrapped in a heavy blue bathrobe and with a blue monk's cowl pulled over his head, he climbed the steps to the ring with the cumbrous agility of a medieval executioner ascending the scaffold.

A.J. Liebling on Rocky Marciano

It was like someone jammed an electric light bulb in your face and busted it. I thought half my head was blowed off.

Jim Braddock on being hit by Joe Louis

He went over like a six-foot sixty-year-old butler who has just heard tragic news.

Norman Mailer on George Foreman hit by Mohammad Ali

Like watching an autopsy on a man who's still alive.

Sylvester Stallone on Mohammad Ali hit by Larry Holmes

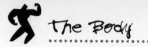 The Body

Football

A bad football team is like an old bra – no cups and little support.

Anon.

I was born for soccer, just as Beethoven was born for music.

Pelé

Brazilian football is like their inflation – 100 per cent.

Jornal da Tarde

Feet as sensitive as a pickpocket's hands.

Hugh McIlvanney on George Best

Vinnie Jones is as discreet as a scream in a cathedral.

Frank McGhee, *The Observer*

Cricket

To the spectators, cricket is more a therapy
than a sport. It is like watching fish dart
about a pool.

Michael Wale

I am to cricket what Dame Sybil Thorndyke
is to nonferrous welding.

Frank Muir

The batsman's technique was like an old lady
poking her umbrella at a wasps' nest.

John Arlott

He approaches the wicket like Groucho
Marx chasing after a pretty waitress.

John Arlott on Asif Masood's bowling action

Tennis

You can't see as well as these fucking flowers
– and they're fucking plastic.

John McEnroe to a line judge

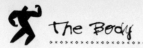

The Benson and Hedges Cup was won by McEnroe ... he was as charming as always, which means that he was as charming as a dead mouse in a loaf of bread.

Clive James

Eddie Izzard: I'm a lesbian trapped in a man's body.
Frank Skinner: A bit like Martina Navratilova.

Frank Skinner Show

It is, perhaps, not too great a trespass against gallantry to point out that Wendy Turnbull is shaped like a Prince Po tennis racket.

Martin Amis

Golf is a game where white men can dress like black pimps and get away with it.

Robin Williams

A golf-course is like a pool-room moved outsides.

Barry Fitzgerald in *Going my Way*, 1949

Watching Sam Snead practise hitting golf balls is like watching a fish practise swimming.

John Schlee

I was swinging like a toilet door on a prawn trawler.

David Feherty

Golf balls are attracted to water as unerringly as the eye of a middle-aged man to a female bosom.

Michael Green, *The Art of Coarse Golf*

The Wrecking Crew were just leaving the eighteenth tee, moving up the fairway with their caddies and looking like one of those great race-migrations of the Middle Ages.

P.G. Wodehouse, *Chester Forgets Himself*

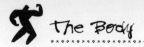

Other Sports

In the steeplechase, Amos Biwott leaped the water jump as if he thought crocodiles were swimming in it.

Joe Henderson

Ocean racing is like standing under a cold shower tearing up £5 notes.

Edward Heath

Most jockeys beat horses as if they were guards in slave-labour camps. Bill Shoemaker treated them as if he were asking them to dance.

Jim Murray, *The Los Angeles Times*

If Jesus Christ rode his flaming donkey like you just rode that horse, then he deserved to be crucified.

Fred Rimell to an amateur jockey

John McCririck looks like Worzel
Gummidge after an incident with a letter
bomb.

Victor Lewis-Smith, *The London Evening Standard*

Dressing a pool player in a tuxedo is like
putting whipped cream on a hot dog.

Minnesota Fats

I was watching Sumo wrestling on the
television for two hours before I realised it
was darts.

Hattie Hayridge

Watching Sumo wrestling from close quarters
is like sitting on the outside of a hairpin bend
during a grand prix for articulated lorries.

Clive James

Grand Prix driving is like balancing an egg
on a spoon while shooting the rapids.

Graham Hill

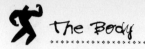

The Body

The driving position is like lying in a bath with your feet on the taps, but not as comfortable.

David Coulthard

Baseball is like watching grass – no, Astroturf grow.

Jeff Jarvis, *Entertainment Weekly*

I felt like I was throwing God out of church.

Drew Coble, umpire, after sending off a star player

If you've only got one day to live, come see the Toronto Maple Leafs. It'll seem like forever.

Pat Foley

Food & Drink

Great food is like great sex – the more you have, the more you want.

Gael Greene

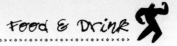

◇<◇><◇><◇><◇><◇><◇><◇><◇><◇><◇><◇><◇><◇><◇><◇><◇><◇>

If only it were as easy to banish hunger by rubbing the belly as it is to masturbate.

Diogenes

Peckish is not the word! I felt like a homeless tapeworm.

P.G. Wodehouse, *Laughing Gas*

A gourmet who thinks of calories is like a tart who looks at her watch.

James Beard

'I liked it, Mom, tasted kind of like chicken.'
'It was chicken.'

Bobby Driscoll and Barbara Hale in *The Window*, 1949

Turkey is totally inedible. It's like eating a scrum half.

Willie Rushton

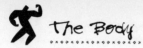 The Body

Surrounded with cold white fat, the rabbit legs looked like maps of Greenland and tasted like a dryad's inner thigh.

Clive James

Gelée of duck had the consistency of Pamela Anderson Lee's implants, and was so salty and horrid it was like licking an Abyssinian shotputter's armpit.

A.A. Gill, *The Sunday Times*

Boiled fish with that awful anchovy sauce that looks as if the cook had bled into it.

Raymond Chandler, *The Long Goodbye*

Eating calf's liver with sauté mushrooms: I've always wondered what it would be like to eat a baby. I think it would taste like this.

Gael Greene

We ate baby vegetables so small it felt like infanticide.

Peter York

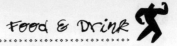

Dried fish is a staple food in Iceland ... It varies in toughness. The tougher kind tastes like toe-nails, and the softer kind like the skin off the soles of one's feet.

W.H. Auden

Gem lettuce frisée looked a bit like the kind of forest you have to hack your way through to reach Sleeping Beauty.

Will Self, *The Observer*

Dog food is an overused amateur description for food and, in the general run of things, I'd steer clear of it, but this plate was so exactly precisely reminiscent of hot Chum that I can really do no better.

A.A. Gill, *The Sunday Times*

Tofu - girls, have you ever had a yeast infection? It's not two hundred miles away from what tofu looks like.

Ruby Wax

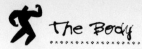

The bread ate as if it had been made by a manic depressive creative therapy class.

A.A. Gill, *The Sunday Times*

The snails still had their horns and were curled up and wrinkled like frost-bitten snotty noses boiled to death in their beds. But the taste was miraculous.

A.A. Gill, *The Sunday Times*

A nectarine – how good how fine. It went down all pulpy, slushy, oozy – all its delicious *embonpoint* melted down my throat like a large, beatified strawberry.

John Keats

Looks like a cross-section through a dead dachshund.

Clive James on Blutwurst, German sausage

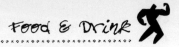
Boiled cabbage à l'Anglaise is something compared with which steamed coarse newsprint bought from bankrupt Finnish salvage dealers and heated over smoky oil stoves is an exquisite delicacy.

William Connor, *The Daily Mirror*

My bowels shall sound like an harp.

Bible, Isaiah 16:2

A steak is every bit as deadly as a gun.

T. Coraghessan Boyle, *The Road to Wellville*

No bigger than your finger, it just lies there innocently like a failed gherkin, but it goes off in your mouth like a petrol bomb. I thought the sun was coming up in my throat.

Clive James on the jalapeño pepper

I bit the head off a live bat the other night. It was like eating a Crunchie wrapped in chamois leather.

Ozzy Osborne

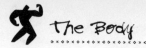

The process of making onion soup is somewhat like love ... commitment, extraordinary
effort, time, and will make you cry.

Ronni Lundy, *Esquire* magazine

Candy bars are like years. We're paying more,
but they're getting shorter.

Charlie Brown

My perfect cake is a cake with icing, but it
must be chocolate and black inside from
chocolate as the devil's arse is black from
smoke. And the icing to be the same.

Marquis de Sade

He imported to the peeling of a banana the
elegant nonchalance of a duke drawing a
monogrammed cigarette from a platinum
case.

Alexander Woolcott, *While Rome Burns*

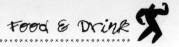

Charles took me to dine at Boulestins. Oysters, red mullet grilled with a slip of banana laid along it like a medieval wife on a tomb.

Sylvia Townsend Warner, *Diaries*

She bore in the Christmas pudding as if it were John the Baptist's head on a plate.

Nicola Zweig

We ate the pudding in respectful silence, as though a coffin were in the room.

Ian Thomson, *The Spectator*

Coffee ... black as the devil, hot as hell, pure as an angel, sweet as sin.

Charles de Talleyrand

English coffee tastes like water that has been squeezed out of a wet sleeve.

Fred Allen

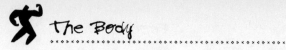

'This coffee tastes like mud,' I said. 'I'm not surprised,' the waitress said, 'it was only ground this morning.'

Les Dawson

Bernie made the kind of tea a mouse could stand on.

Liza Cody, *Dupe*

Sometimes it tastes like water and sometimes like beer, it's never the same.

Sarah Miles on drinking her own urine, (for medicinal purposes)

Jesus, look at that fridge. It was like the laboratory of Sir Alexander Fleming. Get your home-made penicillin here.

William McIlvanney, *The Kiln*

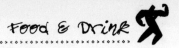
I don't know why I find it intensely erotic to stand naked before an open fridge, but I do... maybe it's that the spill of light on my body makes me feel like a professional stripper.

Stephen Fry, *Making History*

Barbecues are like overhead projectors: they never work first time.

Digby Anderson, *The Spectator*

Putting your name to this place is on a par with Thomas Crapper naming a toilet after himself.

A.A. Gill on The Hempel, restaurant, *The Sunday Times*

Some of the waiters discuss the menu with you as if they were sharing wisdom picked up in the Himalayas.

Seymour Britchky, *The Restaurants of New York*

The food was as tastefully forgettable as ... as ... oh, I can't remember.

A.A. Gill, *The Sunday Times*

Spud-U-Like: like the DSS with potatoes.

Victoria Wood

The eighty-five cent dinner tasted like a
discarded mail bag and was served to me by
a waiter who looked as if he would slug me
for a quarter, cut my throat for six bits, and
bury me at sea in a barrel of concrete for a
dollar and a half, plus sales tax.

Raymond Chandler, Farewell My Lovely

Marks & Spencer makes me think of the
Church, since wherever you go there it is,
completely familiar and offering the same
services.

Alice Thomas Ellis

Visited the food hall at M&S ... Check-out
like the check-in at a gay disco.

Derek Jarman, Modern Nature

Alcohol

The mind is like a flower, it is beautiful
when it is open. The pub is like a flower ...

Sean Hughes, *The Grey Area*

It was like walking into a lung. A sulphur-
stained nicotine-yellow and fly-blown lung.

Paul McGann on a pub in *Withnail and I*, 1987

Smoke-filled, with a smell of testosterone
hanging in the air like the balls of beer.

Stanley Elkin on bars, *The Washington Post*

He tottered blindly towards the bar like a
camel making for an oasis after a hard day at
the office.

P.G. Wodehouse, *Life With Freddie*

Ale flowed like a leak in the Pacific.

Les Dawson

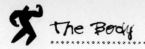
The Body

Drinks flowed like cement.

John Mortimer

Alcohol is like love ... The first kiss is magic,
the second is intimate, the third is routine.
After that you take the girl's clothes off.

Raymond Chandler, *The Long Goodbye*

She sipped her drink as if it had been
poured out for her by a Borgia.

Monica Dickens, *One Pair of Feet*

Drinking raw Absinthe is like swallowing a
Bengal tiger.

Sylvia Townsend Warner, *Diaries*

Connoisseurs who like martinis very dry
suggest simply allowing a ray of sunlight to
shine through a bottle of vermouth before it
hits the bottle of gin – like the Immaculate
Conception.

Luis Buñuel

Exquisite, this little mulled wine! It's like the Good Lord himself slipping down your throat, in red velvet breeches!

Pièrre Brasseur in *Les Enfants du Paradis*, 1945

I sipped the cognac. It tasted like semi-viscous airplane fuel from the Amelia Earhart era.

Kinky Friedman, *When the Cat's Away*

The Spanish wine, my God, it is foul, catpiss is champagne compared, this is the sulphurous urination of some aged horse.

D.H. Lawrence

Château Fleet Street claret ... the metallic flavour of this particular claret gives it a slight prison flavour as if the grape had been grown on the sunless side of Wormwood Scrubs.

John Mortimer

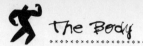
Hangover

God, what on earth was I drinking last night? My head feels like there's a Frenchman living in it.

Blackadder II

I woke up with the kind of headache you'd get if you'd been drinking cheap champagne from a size-14 Cinderella slipper.

Kinky Friedman, *Frequent Flyer*

I felt pretty good – like an amputated leg.

Dick Powell in *Farewell My Lovely*, 1944

My mouth is so dry they could shoot Lawrence of Arabia in it.

Dyan Cannon in *The Last of Sheila*, 1973

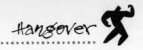

Try opening your eyes. It's like when you were young and you used to take the cellophane wrapper from a Quality Street toffee and hold it over your eyes ...

Stephen Fry, *Making History*

I smelled of gin. Not just casually, as if I had taken four or five drinks of a winter morning to get out of bed on, but as if the Pacific Ocean was pure gin and I had nose-dived off the boat deck.

Raymond Chandler, *The Lady in the Lake*

Being drunk is like having a moustache. It looks good on a man and terrible on a woman.

Tony Parsons, *Arena* magazine

Vices

'How do I look?'
'Like a woman about to go forth and sin.'
'Good, just the look I was trying for.'

Cher and Winona Ryder in *Mermaids*, 1990

She smoked a hundred and twenty gaspers a day, swore like a fisherman, drank like a fish, and was promiscuous with men, women and Etonians.

Quentin Crisp

I'm as pure as the driven slush.

Tallulah Bankhead

I lit a cigarette. It tasted like a plumber's handkerchief.

Raymond Chandler, *Farewell My Lovely*

Cigarette smoke came like spectral tusks
from his nostrils.

Martin Amis, *Other People*

I puffed at the cigarette. It was one of those
things with filters in them. It tasted like a
high fog strained through cotton wool.

Raymond Chandler, *The Long Goodbye*

I toil after it, sir, as some men toil after
virtue.

Charles Lamb on being asked how he could smoke so many
cigars

Ecstasy – a drug white people take to make
them think they can dance like black people.

Lenny Henry

Many tiny jewelled violet flowers along the
path of a living brook that looked like
Blake's illustration for a canal in grassy Eden.

Allen Ginsberg describing an LSD trip

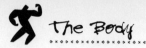 The Body

There is hardly a chic party given nowadays
that doesn't sound like a hay fever clinic
during the month of June.

Taki on cocaine, *The Spectator*

Taking cocaine is like being a haemophiliac
in a razor factory.

Robin Williams

I'll die young, but it's like kissing God.

Lennie Bruce

People

Men

They act like God Almighty, 'cos they've got
a cock, and they can mend a flex.

Victoria Wood

Deep down inside, they are biological
creatures, like jellyfish or trees, only less
likely to clean the bathroom.

Dave Barry, *Dave Barry's Complete Guide to Guys*

Some men just naturally make you think of
brut champagne. With others, you think of
prune juice.

Barbara Lawrence in *Unfaithfully Yours*, 1948

I'd like to get to the point where I can be
just as mediocre as a man.

Juanita Kreps

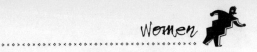

Men are like car alarms. They both make a
lot of noise no one listens to.

Diana Jordan and Paul Scaburn

What a nasty mind you have, Bruce. Where
did you learn to think like a woman?

Frank G. Slaughter, War Surgeon

Women

Why can't a woman be more like a man?

Rex Harrison in My Fair Lady, 1964

Were there no women, men might live like
gods.

Thomas Dekker

 The Body

In various stages of her life, a woman
resembles the continents of the world. From
13 to 18, she's like Africa – virgin territory;
from 18 to 30, she's like Asia – hot and
exotic; from 30 to 45, she's like America –
fully explored and free with her resources;
from 45 to 55, she's like Europe – exhausted,
but not without places of interest; after 55,
she's like Australia – everybody knows it's
down there, but nobody much cares.

Al Boliska

Women are like elephants to me: I like to
look at them, but I wouldn't want to own
one.

W.C. Fields

All women become like their mothers, that
is their tragedy. No man ever does. That is
his.

Oscar Wilde

There is no sin like being a woman.

Quentin Crisp

There is no sincerity like a woman telling a lie.

Cecil Parker in *Indiscreet*, 1958

Certain women should be struck regularly, like gongs.

Noel Coward

I look on the sex with something like the admiration with which I regard the starry sky in a frosty December night. I admire the beauty of the Creator's workmanship; I am charmed with the wild but graceful eccentricity of their motions; and – wish them both goodnight.

Robert Burns

Dating – her view

There is no fury like a woman searching for a new lover.

Cyril Connolly

Finding a man is like finding a job; it's easier to find one when you already have one.

Paige Mitchell

'What's your new boyfriend like?'
'Did you ever see *Officer and a Gentleman*?
Well, he's kinda like the guy I went to see that with.'

Friends, US sitcom

He makes Frankenstein look like a lily.

Glenda Farrell in *The Mystery of the Wax Museum*, 1933

He's like a cold, and there are only two things you can do with a cold. You can fight it or you can go to bed with it. I'm going to fight it.

Doris Day in *Lover Come Back*, 1961

She seems to attract the sort of man who looks as if he keeps pigeons.

The Observer

'During this time of the year these slippery little creatures come up on the beach, stop, spawn and then go out to sea again.'
'Sounds like some naval officers I know.'
Anne Francis and Companion in *Don't Go Near the Water*, 1957

Men like to pursue an elusive woman, like a cake of wet soap in a bathtub.

Gelett Burgess

Men, I feel, are like wine – before buying, a real connoisseur takes a small sip and spits them out.

Jill Tweedie

I eat men like air.

Sylvia Plath

There are men one goes through like countries.

Jeanne Moreau, well-travelled French actress

Valerie fondles men like a mousetrap fondles mice.

Roger McGough, *Discretion*

The little moth round candle turning,
Stops not till its wings are burning:
So woman, dazzled by man's wooing,
Rushes to her own undoing.

Charlotte Dacre

I am waiting for the phone again ... Feel as if I have just sat an exam and must wait for my results.

Helen Fielding after a first date, *Bridget Jones's Diary*

My Dear One is mine as mirrors are lonely.

W.H. Auden

Only time can heal your broken heart, just like only time can heal his broken arms and legs.

Miss Piggy

Dating – his view

Treat a whore like a lady and a lady like a whore.

Wilson Mizner

 *People*

You are only allowed three great women in your lifetime. They come along like the great fighters. Once every ten years.

Chazz Palminteri in A Bronx Tale, 1993

She's amazing! She makes the women that I dream about look like short, fat, bald men.

Friends, US sitcom

All other women are like the second pressing of the grape.

John Wayne in The Conqueror, 1956

She looked like a woman you might jump a few lights to get home to.

William McIlvanney, The Papers of Tony Veitch

I want you like people in hell want ice water.

Ed Harris in Sweet Dreams, 1985

I want to climb inside you and pull you around me like a blanket.

Richard Dreyfuss in The Competition, 1980

◇◇

Women are like banks, boy. Breaking and entering is a serious business.

> Joe Orton

I'll meet you tonight under the moon. Oh, I can see you now – you and the moon. You wear a necktie so I'll know you.

Groucho Marx to Margaret Dumont in *The Cocoanuts,* 1929

It's nights like this that drive men like me to women like you for nights like this.

> Bob Hope in *My Favorite Spy*, 1951

I had a great time tonight, really. It was like the Nuremberg Trials.

> Woody Allen, *Hannah and her Sisters*, 1986

I like her from a distance ... you know, the way you like the sun. Maris is like the sun – except without the warmth.

> *Frasier*, US sitcom

 People

She has a shoulder that would make dry ice feel like a bed warmer.

Melvyn Douglas in *This Thing Called Love*, 1941

I dropped her like a bad habit.

James Crumley

I need you as much as I need a giraffe.

William Powell in *The Ex-Mrs Bradford*, 1936

Nothing in the world is as hopeful as knowing a woman you like is somewhere thinking about only you.

Richard Ford

Life without you was like a broken pencil ... pointless.

Blackadder II

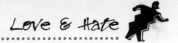
Love & Hate

When the moon hits your eye
Like a big pizza pie,
That's Amore ...

> Dean Martin, *That's Amore*

Love can leave you reeling faster than a one-eyed cat in a fish market.

> Felicia R. Lee, *The New York Times*

To fall in love you have to be in a state of mind for it to take, like a disease.

> Nancy Mitford

Love, like poetry, is a kind of homesickness, the kind which made medieval monks sleep in their coffins.

> Jennifer Stone, *Nostalgia*

 People

Love is much nicer to be in than an
automobile accident, a tight girdle, a
higher tax bracket or a holding pattern
over Philadelphia.

Judith Viorst

It's like eating strawberries and cream in a
new dress by moonlight, on a summer night,
while somebody plays the violin far away in
the distance so that you can just hear it.

P.G. Wodehouse, *The Prince and Betty*

We feasted on love, every mode of it –
solemn and merry, romantic as a thunder-
storm, sometimes as comfortable and
unemphatic as putting on your slippers.

C.S. Lewis

Was that cannon fire – or is it my heart
pounding?

Ingrid Bergman in *Casablanca*, 1942

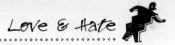
We made love as though we were an endangered species.

Peter de Vries

He made love faster than the time it takes to get a vaccination.

Frasier, US sitcom

Ill-conceived love is like a Christmas cracker – one massively disappointing bang and the novelty soon wears off.

Blackadder's Christmas Carol

My love is like a red, red rose – expensive and hard to handle.

Anon.

Love is a great glue, but there is no cement like mutual hate.

Loise Wyse, *The Rosemary Touch*

Hate fills my mouth like spit.

Margaret Atwood

I hate you like all-fire.

Truman Capote

'I hate it,' she said. 'I hate it like I hate the sunshine and the summer and the bright stars and the full moon. That's how I hate it.'

Raymond Chandler, *Playback*

Kissing

'I've got a funny sensation in my toes, like someone was barbecuing them over a slow flame.'
'Let's throw another log on the fire.'

Tony Curtis and Marilyn Monroe in *Some Like it Hot*, 1959

Like kissing Hitler.

Tony Curtis on Marilyn Monroe

Like kissing the Berlin Wall.

Helena Bonham Carter on Woody Allen

When women kiss it always reminds me of

prize-fighters shaking hands.

H. L. Mencken

So, you want a hickey ... Buy me a Mercedes
and I'll make your neck look like a relief
map of the Andes.

Frasier, US sitcom

How about a Spanish kiss under the
mistletoe? It's like a French kiss only a little
further south.

Anon.

Kissing is pretty much like an opening act.
It's like a stand-up comedian you have to sit
through before Pink Floyd comes out.

Friends, US sitcom

Sex

It's great stuff, like chocolate sundaes.

Raymond Chandler, *The Little Sister*

Sex is like money; only too much is enough.

John Updike

Two minutes of gooey near-satisfaction followed by weeks of haunting guilt is so much
more easily attained at Haagen-Däzs

Florence Campbell

Conventional sexual intercourse is like
squirting jam into a doughnut.

Germaine Greer

Foreplay is like beefburgers – three minutes
on each side.

Victoria Wood

Sex with me is like nuclear war – when I'm done, there's nothing left standing.

Cybill, US sitcom

She tore her clothes off like a nun forsaking her vows.

Peter de Vries, *The Prick of Noon*

Their bodies raged like an apocalypse of fire, pleasure and small-time perversion.

Richard Brautigan, *Willard and his Bowling Trophies*

A multiple orgasm is like a good stereo – something you see in magazines and which other people have.

Jeremy Hardy, *Jeremy Hardy Speaks to the Nation*

The American women I know all talk about 'having sex'; they say things like 'We had great sex' as if it were Chinese food or good weather.

Lucretia Stewart, *Punch*

 People

My husband and I had our best sex during the divorce. It was like cheating on our lawyers.

Priscilla Lopez in *Cheaper to Keep Her*, 1981

Despite a lifetime of service to the cause of sexual liberation, I have never caught a venereal disease, which makes me feel rather like an Arctic explorer who has never had frostbite.

Germaine Greer

Seven inches long and three times as wide as a normal condom — a clear polyurethane sheath strangely reminiscent of an icing bag, or a rain hat for a small wizard.

Helen Fielding on the female condom, *The Sunday Times*

New coil inserted. Recall Edward II disembowelled at Berkeley Castle.

Sue Limb, *Dulcie Domum's Bad Housekeeping*

It is good to be chaste, like a river of cold
water in the soul.

D.H. Lawrence, *Lady Chatterley's Lover*

Asking me if I'm homosexual is a little like
asking a man crawling across the Sahara
whether he would prefer Perrier or Malvern
water.

Alan Bennett

Straight? He's about as straight as the Yellow
Brick Road.

Laurence Luckinbill in *The Boys in the Band*, 1970

A woman reading *Playboy* feels a little like a
Jew reading a Nazi manual.

Gloria Steinem

Pornography is rather like trying to find out
about a Beethoven Symphony by having
someone tell you about it and perhaps hum
a few bars.

Robertson Davies

Have a wank? It would be easier to raise the *Titanic*.

Alfred Molina in *Prick Up Your Ears*, 1987

Sex at 93 is like playing billiards with a rope.

George Burney

It's like being unchained from a lunatic.

Sophocles on his declining sexual powers

Weddings

A lot like childbirth, you remember the joy, not the pain.

The New York Times

Having a wedding without mentioning divorce is like sending someone to war without mentioning that people are going to get killed.

Richard Curtis, *Four Weddings and a Funeral*

Weddings

◇>◇<◇>◇<◇>◇<◇>◇<◇>◇<◇>◇<◇>◇<◇>◇<◇>◇<◇>◇<◇>◇<◇>◇<◇>◇<◇>◇<◇

She looked like one of those dolls used to
hide spare toilet rolls.

Cosmopolitan magazine on bride, Danni Minogue

The wedding veil makes her look as if she's
been mugged by a pair of net curtains.

Victoria Wood

No matter what kind of music you ask them
to play, they'll play it in such a way that it
sounds like *New York, New York*.

Dave Barry on wedding bands

Married five times? Wedding bells must
sound like an alarm clock to you.

Mae West in *I'm no Angel*, 1933

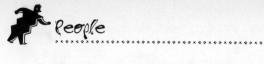
Marriage & Divorce

Marriage, well, I think it's a marvellous thing for other people, like going to the stake.

Philip Larkin

Sex is for men, and marriage, like lifeboats, is for women and children.

Carrie Fisher, *Surrender the Pink*

Marriage is forever. It's like cement.

Peter O'Toole in *What's New Pussycat?*, 1965

Marriage is like the Middle East. There's no solution.

Pauline Collins in *Shirley Valentine*, 1989

My marriage with Bill was like a close-up of tooth decay.

Roseanne, *Roseanne, My Lives*

The pain of death is nothing compared to the pain of sharing a coffeepot with a peevish woman.

John Cheever on his wife, Mary

They kept mistresses of such dowdiness they might almost have been mistaken for wives.

Robertson Davies

Being a mistress is like having a book out from the library.

Lorrie Moore, *How to Be an Other Woman*

I'm old-fashioned. I don't believe in extra-marital relationships. I think people should mate for life, like pigeons and Catholics.

Woody Allen and Marshall Brickman, *Manhattan*, 1979

Getting divorced is like getting hit by a Mack truck. If you live through it, you start looking very carefully to the right and to the left.

Jean Kerr

Being a divorcee in a small town is a little like playing Monopoly; eventually you land on all the properties.

John Updike

My father came and went like the tide.

Olivia Harris

If I turn into my parents, I'll either be an alcoholic blonde chasing twenty-year-old boys or... I'll wind up like my mother.

Friends, US sitcom

Children

'Why do you want children, Dorothy?'
'I don't know why, Gary, I just want them. It's like you and lager.'

Men Behaving Badly, sitcom

A male gynaecologist is like an auto mechanic who never owned a car.

Carrie Snow

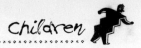
My female friends had told me that giving birth was like shitting a water melon. They lied. It's like excreting a block of flats – complete with patios, awnings, clothes-lines, television aerials, satellite dishes, backyard barbecues, kidney-shaped swimming pools, gazebos and double garage extensions with the cars parked outside.

Kathy Lette, Foetal Attraction

Giving birth is like sitting on top of the Eiffel Tower and spinning.

Ruby Wax

Having a baby is like watching two very inefficient removal men trying to get a very large sofa through a very small doorway, only in this case you can't say, 'Oh, sod it, bring it through the French windows.'

Victoria Wood

It was one of those bulging babies. It looked a little like Boris Karloff and a little like Winston Churchill.

P.G. Wodehouse

 People

My baby's got a mouth like a staple-gun.
> Breast feeding mother, *ER*, TV medical drama

Bridget ... romped on my lap like a short stout salmon.
> Sylvia Townsend Warner, *Diaries*

People who say they sleep like a baby usually don't have one.
> Leo J. Burke

When you're the only pea in the pod your parents are likely to get you confused with the Hope Diamond.
> Russell Baker

Real mothers think sex is like full-time employment – it's a nice idea but it'll never happen again in their lifetime.
> Victoria Wood

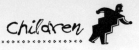
Cleaning your house while your children are still growing is like shovelling the walk before it stops snowing.

Phyllis Diller

Kids are like husbands – they're fine as long as they're someone else's.

Marsha Warfield

Life &
Death

Life

'Life is like that, dear,' she would sometimes say, but she would never say what it was that life was like.

Ronald Firbank

Life is rather like opening a tin of sardines. We're all of us looking for the key.

Alan Bennett

Life is like a little strip of pavement over an abyss.

Virginia Woolf

Life is like jaywalking at Le Mans.

William McIlvanney, *The Big Man*

Life is like Sanskrit read to a pony.

Lou Reed

Life is like a sewer. What you get out of it depends upon what you put in.

Tom Lehrer

Nothing in life ever looks as good as it does on the seed packet.

Kinky Friedman, *Elvis, Jesus and Coca-Cola*

They say movies should be more like life. I think life should be more like the movies.

Myrna Loy

It's a good thing that life is not as serious as it seems to a waiter.

Don Herold

I'm pretty sure I'm dying and my purpose is to hang on to life. Like grim death.

Jeffrey Bernard, *The Spectator*

Death

Nothing is as certain as death and taxes.

Benjamin Franklin

There are worse things in life than death. Think of death as cutting down on your expenses.

Woody Allen, *Love and Death*, 1975

It was death – possibly the only dinner guest more unwelcome than Sidney Poitier.

Kinky Friedman, *When the Cat's Away*

'What's death like?'
'It's as bad as the chicken at Tresky's Restaurant.'

Woody Allen, *Love and Death*, 1975

Death is like the rumble of distant thunder at a picnic.

W.H. Auden

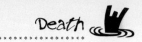

Death is very sophisticated. It's like a Noel Coward comedy. You light a cigarette and wait for it in the library.

Theadora Van Runkle

'Dying is like falling off a cliff. You've never fallen off a cliff in your life, have you, Ollie?' 'Yes, I did. When I met you.'

Ali McGraw and Ryan O'Neal in *Love Story*, 1970

Arthur died ... one minute I was talking to my agent and the next thing he was gone. It's like ten per cent of me died.

Cybill, US sitcom

The funeral reception ... Like the wedding only less white.

Dressing for Breakfast, sitcom

Death, like life, is too serious a subject to be taken solemnly.

C. Murray Parkes

Religion

It's just as Christian to go down on your
knees for sex as it is for religion.

Larry Flynt

Nuns go by as quiet as lust.

Toni Morrison, *The Bluest Eye*

Everyone would like to behave like a pagan,
with everyone else behaving like a Christian.

Albert Camus

Pastor Spratt was very impressive. My mother
said he looked like Errol Flynn, but holy.

Jeanette Winterson, *Oranges Are Not the Only Fruit*

Sir, a woman preaching is like a dog walking
on its hind legs. You don't expect it to be
done well – you are surprised to find it done
at all.

Samuel Johnson

A woman's asking for equality in the church would be comparable to a black person's demanding equality in the Ku Klux Klan.

Mary Daly

She fought off God like an unwelcome suitor.

Nancy Evans

The New English Bible: even the end of the world is described as if it were only an exceptionally hot afternoon.

Peter Mallen

Life after death is as improbable as sex after marriage.

Madeline Kahn in *Clue*, 1985

The World

The world is like a cucumber; today it's in your hands, tomorrow it's up your arse.

Arabic proverb

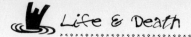

The universe is like a safe to which there is a combination – but the combination is locked up in the safe.

Peter de Vries

The world lay all before me – like a trap-door.

Quentin Crisp

I wish I could possess the world as I possess a woman.

Aleksandr Scriabin

You stand on the brink of greatness. The world will open up to you like an oyster, no, no, not like an oyster ... the world will open up to you like a magnificent vagina.

Woody Allen and Douglas McGrath, *Bullets Over Broadway*, 1994

Age

I swear I'm aging about as well as a beach–
party movie.

> Harvey Fierstein in *Torch Song Trilogy*, 1988

I've aged! There are new lines on my face. I
look like a brand new, steel-belted radial
tyre.

> Maggie Smith in *California Suite*, 1978

I look like Barbara Cartland without the
vitamins.

> Victoria Wood

Like a hole in the head I need another
birthday

> Dorothy Parker, *The Middle of Blue Period*

Being a balding fortysomething chap with bad teeth and a young pretty girlfriend is the social equivalent of wearing a chest wig, a medallion, dyeing your hair and driving an E-Type Jaguar with Barry White full blast on the stereo.

A.A. Gill, *The Sunday Times*

Growing old is like being increasingly penalized for a crime you haven't committed.

Anthony Powell

There are people who are beautiful in dilapidation, like houses that were hideous when new.

Logan Pearsall Smith

Like all good ruins, I look better by moonlight.

Anon.

Intelligence

'Your brain is like the four-headed man-eating haddock fish-beast of Aberdeen.'
'In what way?'
'It doesn't exist.'

Blackadder's Christmas Carol

Nature had not given her more than about as much brain as would fit comfortably into an aspirin bottle.

P.G. Wodehouse, *Galahad at Blandings*

Americans invented the dumb broad as the English perfected the gun dog.

John Osborne

Your head is as empty as a eunuch's underpants.

Blackadder's Christmas Carol

I was the intellectual equivalent of a 98-pound weakling. I'd go to the beach and people would kick copies of Byron in my face.

Robin Williams in *Dead Poets Society*, 1989

The lesson of anatomy applies: there is nothing so rare as the normal.

Somerset Maugham on the incidence of genius

Human Nature & Behaviour

People shouldn't be treated like objects. They're not that valuable.

P.J. O'Rourke

Good taste and humour are a contradiction in terms, like a chaste whore.

Malcolm Muggeridge

Trust is like virginity, you can lose it only once.

Robert Maxwell

I felt as welcome as a fart in a spacesuit.

Billy Connolly

He's as popular as rabies in a guide dogs' home.

Anon.

I'm as busy as a one-armed taxi-driver with crabs.

Sir Les Patterson

As exciting as a weekend at Malaga airport.

Will Woodward, *Time Out*

Hipper than colonic irrigation.

Iain Sinclair, *Radon's Daughters*

Her flamboyance made the Gabor sisters look like *Little Women*.

John Richardson, *Vanity Fair*

He's as sensitive as a goddam toilet seat.

J.D. Salinger, *The Catcher in the Rye*

I've got to urinate like a racehorse.

Kinky Friedman, *When the Cat's Away*

Stand rigid, staring intently ahead, as though the wall tiles were inscribed with a secret formula for turning Grape Nuts into platinum. DEATH BEFORE EYE CONTACT, that is the motto of a guy at a public urinal.

Dave Barry's *Complete Guide to Guys*

The fearful symmetry of this decision struck me like a lump of frozen urine from an airliner flying low over West London.

Michael Vestey, *The Spectator*

Every decision is like murder and our march forward is over the stillborn bodies of all our possible selves that will never be.

René Dubos

◇◆◇◆◇◆◇◆◇◆◇◆◇◆◇◆◇◆◇◆◇◆◇◆◇◆◇◆◇◆◇◆◇◆◇

Like a lonely fishfinger I lie in bed pulling
the breadcrumbs over my head.

Greetings card message

She fastened on to her with the enthusiasm
of a lonely tsetse fly encountering an outpost
of civilization.

Saki

She recurs like onions.

Edith Sitwell

Lady Badbreath, fresh as stilton ...

Cyril Connolly

Aloof, like Lady Nevershit ...

Arnold Wesker

As a source of entertainment, conviviality
and good fun, she ranks somewhere between
a sprig of parsley and a single ice-skate...She
is about as hot company as a night nurse.

Dorothy Parker, *Wallflower's Lament*

I tried to be pleasant and chatty. It was like engaging the pyramids in small talk.

Somerset Maugham

She is as quiet as a wasp in one's ear

Thomas Fuller

Her nagging is kinda like living near the airport – after a while you don't notice it any more.

Roseanne, US sitcom

He was drooping as if he had been stuffed in a hurry by an incompetent taxidermist.

P.G. Wodehouse, *The Mating Season*

I'm as soft as a sneaker full of slime.

Kurt Vonnegut

I'm as nervous as a virgin at a prison rodeo.

The Golden Girls, US sitcom

I'm as comfortable as a lame turkey sat on a pile of Paxo listening to Christmas Carols.

Les Dawson

He looked like a man who's just realised that he's posted a love letter in the wrong envelope.

Hugh Laurie, *The Gun Seller*

Worry is like a rocking chair. It gives you something to do, but it doesn't get you anywhere.

Anon.

I turned to Aunt Agatha, whose demeanour was now rather like that of one who, picking daisies on the railway, has just caught the down express in the small of her back.

P.G. Wodehouse, *The Inimitable Jeeves*

She was looking about as pale as a beetroot that has suddenly heard bad news.

Saki

She blushed like a well-trained sunset.

Margaret Halsey

'You came in here as white as a sheet and
now you are as purple as ...'
'A purple sheet.'

Stephen Fry, *Making History*

Happiness &
Unhappiness

Happiness descended upon her heart, like a
cloud of morning dew in a dell of flowers.

Walter De La Mare

'This,' he said, 'is like being in heaven without going to all the bother and expense of
dying.'

P.G. Wodehouse, *Hot Water*

Many in this world run after felicity like an
absent-minded man hunting for his hat
while all the time it is on his head.

Sydney Smith

I'm as happy as the day is long. The day in
question being January. Somewhere inside
the Arctic Circle.

Victor Lewis-Smith, *The London Evening Standard*

He stood there looking as sad as a dead bird's
bird-bath.

Georg Christoph Lichtenberg

He had a face like a requiem.

Honoré de Balzac

A melancholy-looking man, had had the
appearance of one who has searched for the
leak in life's gas-pipe with a lighted candle.

P.G. Wodehouse, *The Man Who Disliked Cats*

He looked, as ever, as cheerful as a tomb-
stone.

Spencer Bright, *The Daily Mail*

Depression sits on my chest like a Sumo wrestler.

Sandra Scoppettone, *I'll be Leaving You Always*

She's like a mourner peeling onions.

Alan Ayckbourn, *Sisterly Feelings*

Between the hours of her rehearsals she visited the cemeteries of Paris and sat among the tombstones like a sister of the departed.

H. and D.L. Thomas on Sarah Bernhardt

Freddie experienced the sort of abysmal soul sadness which afflicts one of Tolstoi's peasants when, after putting in a heavy day's work strangling his father, beating his wife, and dropping the baby into the city reservoir, he turns to the cupboard, only to find the vodka bottle empty.

P.G. Wodehouse, *Jill the Reckless*

Rich & Poor

I was born into money and there was
nothing I could do about it. It was there,
like air or food, or any other element.

John D. Rockefeller, Jr

Money, it turned out, was exactly like sex;
you thought of nothing else if you didn't
have it and thought of other things if you
did.

James Baldwin

A man being rich is like a girl being pretty.
You might not marry her just because she's
pretty, but goodness, doesn't it help?

Marilyn Monroe in *Gentlemen Prefer Blondes*, 1953

Money and love, in one respect they're alike.
They're both wonderful as long as they last.

Abigail Van Buren

The real tragedy of the poor is that they can afford nothing but self-denial. Beautiful sins, like beautiful things, are the privilege of the rich.

Oscar Wilde

I'd like to live like a poor man with lots of money.

Pablo Picasso

If you're going to make money, you have to look like money.

'Diamond Jim' Brady

He makes money like rabbits make rabbits.

Anon.

An unsightly bulge of notes in Askead's pocket, snug as a colostomy bag.

Iain Sinclair, *Radon's Daughters*

Money is like manure. You have to spread it around or it smells.

John Paul Getty

He threw his money about like a man with
no arms.

William McIlvanney, *The Papers of Tony Veitch*

You throw money around like it was money.

John Ireland in *All the King's Men*, 1949

His wallet is more capacious than an
elephant's scrotum and just as difficult to get
your hands on.

Blackadder II

He makes Scrooge look like a public bene-
factor.

Anon.

A bellperson carries my luggage – one small
gym-style bag ... and I tip him $2, which he
takes as if I am handing him a jar of warm
sputum.

Dave Barry, *Dave Barry's Greatest Hits*

She gave him her nickel with the manner of
one presenting a park to the city.

Dorothy Parker on tipping

I have a lust for diamonds, almost like a disease.

Elizabeth Taylor

Eva Peron lifted her hands to the crowd, and as she did so, with a sound like railway coaches in a siding, the diamond bracelets slid from her wrists to her armpits. When the expensive clatter had died away, her speech began, 'We, the shirtless ...'

Quentin Crisp, *How to Have a Life-Style*

Nature

Wildlife

A horse, like Cary Grant, lends romance to
any venture.

> Roberta Smoodin, *The New York Times*

A camel looks like a horse that was planned
by a committee.

> *Vogue*

Did you ever see anything that reminded
you so much of a dowager duchess studying
hoi polloi through a gold-rimmed lorgnette?

> Fyfe Robertson on a camel

Honey, there's a spider in the bathroom the
size of a Buick.

> Woody Allen and Marshall Brickman, *Annie Hall*, 1977

The tortoise is the animal equivalent of a
Tonka toy.

> Nick Hancock

◇×◇

Do you recollect the Alington poodle?
Exactly like a typhoid germ magnified.

George Lyttelton

Sportif, they scratch their itches
like one-legged cyclists sprinting
for home, pee like hurdlers,
shit like weightlifters ...

Craig Raine, *The Behaviour of Dogs*

The dog was licking its private parts with
the gusto of an alderman drinking soup.

Graham Greene

I wish they were like the White Rhino – six
of them left in the Serengeti National Park
and all males.

Alan Bennett on dogs

Dogs cannot answer back, they're like royalty

Sue Townsend, *The Secret Diary of Adrian Mole aged 13 3/4*

Among wolves, howl like a wolf.

Russian proverb

No one's ever actually called a cat. Like experienced lovers, they come when they wish.

Kinky Friedman, *Elvis, Jesus and Coca-Cola*

I do not consider pigeons birds. They are more in the nature of people; people who mooch.

Robert Benchley

Have you ever pondered on the similarity between a pelican and British gas? They can both stick their bills up their arses.

Stephen Fry

He followed me like an unpaid bill.

Myrtle Reed on her pet goat

Short, potbellied penguins, whose necks wobbled with baby fat, huddled together like Russian businessmen in fur coats.

Diane Ackerman, *The Moon by Whale Light*

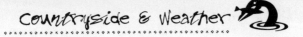
The floorboards had squeaked like mice as I climbed into bed, and the mice between the walls had creaked like wood.

Dylan Thomas, *A Visit to Grandpa's*

Nutkin danced up and down like a sunbeam.

Beatrix Potter, *The Tale of Squirrel Nutkin*

To catch a squirrel, make a noise like a nut.

Anon.

Countryside & Weather

In the afternoons I sat there with my long, iced drink feeling like a pissed badger who'd gatecrashed a Beatrix Potter party.

Jeffrey Bernard on a weekend in the country, *The Spectator*

 Nature

He worked like hell in the country so he could live in the city, where he worked like hell so he could live in the country.

Don Marquis

It looked more like a field of heather than a field of heather.

William Wyler on Hollywood's re-creation of the Yorkshire Moors for *Wuthering Heights*

The sun was like a huge fifty-cent piece that someone had poured kerosene on and then had lit with a match and said, 'Here, hold this while I go get a newspaper,' and put the coin in my hand, but never come back.

Richard Brautigan, *Trout Fishing in America*

The heat was like a hand on the face all day and night.

Josephine W. Johnson, *Now in November*

A few summers like this and we'll all be behaving like Italians.

The Listener on an English heatwave

That night it rained like a bitch with a charge account.

Kinky Friedman, *Greenwich Killing Time*

Rain fell as if an expensive postal address gave you no privileges at all.

Clive James, *Brilliant Creatures*

The rain was gusting against the window as if propelled by a trainee special effects man.

Kingsley Amis

I'm dreaming of a white Christmas, just like the ones I used to know ...

Bing Crosby, *White Christmas*

The snow sounded as if someone was kissing the window all over outside.

Lewis Carroll

March – the month that shows people who don't drink exactly how a hangover feels.

Garrison Keillor

... fog as thick as phlegm

Craig Raine, *Meditation at Spring Hill*

A dim Scottish sun is out, less day realised
than day potential, as if God has left on the
pilot light.

William McIlvanney, *The Kiln*

The afternoon was cold as blue eyes that
didn't love you anymore.

Kinky Friedman, *When the Cat's Away*

Let us go then, you and I,
When the evening is spread out against the
sky
Like a patient etherised upon a table...

T.S. Eliot, *The Love Song of J. Alfred Prufrock*

The evening was beautiful and crisp, just
beginning to chill like a fine imported wine.
Or a freshly croaked stiff.

Kinky Friedman, *Greenwich Killing Time*

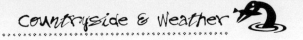
It was as dark as the inside of a Cabinet Minister.

Joyce Cary, *The Horse's Mouth*

The moon looks like a fingernail-cutting...

Colette

I was sat at the bottom of the garden a week ago, smoking a reflective cheroot, thinking about this and that – mostly that, and I just happened to glance at the night sky and I marvelled at the millions of stars glistening like pieces of quicksilver thrown carelessly onto black velvet. In awe I watched the waxen moon ride across the zenith of the heavens like an amber chariot towards the void of infinite space wherein the tethered bolts of Jupiter and Mars hang forever festooned in their orbital majesty, and as I looked at all this, I thought, 'I must put a roof on this lavatory.'

Les Dawson

Travel

Places

England is like an old gentleman who
married late in life, and married his cook.

Sylvia Townsend Warner, *Diaries*

Brighton looks like it's permanently helping
the police with its enquiries.

Keith Waterhouse

The great thing about Glasgow now is that if
there's a nuclear attack it'll look exactly the
same afterwards.

Billy Connolly

The trees are like candelabra. The pastries
like art.

Lorrie Moore on Paris, *Who Will Run the Frog Hospital?*

Paris is like a whore. From a distance she seems ravishing, you can't wait until you have her in your arms. And five minutes later you feel empty, disgusted with yourself. You feel tricked.

Henry Miller, *Tropic of Cancer*

The sunshine had the density of gold-leaf: we seemed to be driving though the landscape of a missal.

Edith Wharton on Italy

Rome reminds me of a man who lives by exhibiting to travellers his grandmother's corpse.

James Joyce

Venice is like eating an entire box of chocolate liqueurs at one go.

Truman Capote

Venice is excessively ugly in the rain – it looks like King's Cross.

John Gielgud

 Travel

Like *Webster's Dictionary*, we're Morocco bound.

> Bob Hope and Bing Crosby in *The Road to Morocco*

Like Torremolinos with guns.

> Anon. on Tel Aviv

I feel about New York as a child whose father is a bank robber ... not perfect, but I still love him.

> Woody Allen

Restaurants look like car washes, car washes look like art galleries, art galleries look like war memorials, war memorials look like fire stations, fire stations look like churches, churches look like restaurants.

> Clive James on Los Angeles

Things are different at night ... Landing at Los Angeles was like landing inside a diamond ring.

> Richard Brautigan

Places

◇•◇

Omaha is a little like Newark – without Newark's glamour.

Joan Rivers

To live in Australia permanently is rather like going to a party and dancing all night with your mother.

Barry Humphries

Living here is like waiting for the funeral to begin. No, it's like waiting in the coffin for them to take you out.

Bette Davis in *Beyond the Forest*, 1949

Don't talk to me about the South Pole – it's like someone telling Noah about a drizzle.

P.G. Wodehouse

Niagara Falls from the air looked like the kitchen sink running over.

Peter de Vries

The Sydney Opera House looks as if it is something that has crawled out of the sea and is up to no good.

Beverley Nichols

the lighthouse stands
like a salt cellar by Magritte

Craig Raine, *The Meteorological Lighthouse at O-*

Public transportation should be avoided with
precisely the same zeal that one accords
Herpes II.

Fran Lebowitz, *Metropolitan Life*

Cabs are like women, or horses, or happiness,
or money, or pet parakeets. If you pursue
them with great ardor you'll never have
them. If you honestly don't give a damn
they'll very often light right on your shoulder,
in which case the pet parakeet is, of course,
preferable to the horse or the cab.

Kinky Friedman, *God Bless John Wayne*

Going by railroad I do not consider as
travelling. It is merely being 'sent' to a place,
and very little different from being a parcel.

John Ruskin

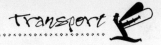
A motorbike is a bit like a horse. If you
don't get on with it, you should get another.

Amanda Garwood, *Harpers and Queen* magazine

As elegant as a swan, nimble as a reed and
finely carved as a violin.

Marlise Simons on a gondola, *The New York Times*

I feel about aeroplanes the way I feel about
diets. They're wonderful things for other
people to go on.

Jean Kerr

Try flying any plane with a baby if you want
a sense of what it must have been like to be
a leper in the fourteenth century.

Nora Ephron, *Heartburn*

Cars

This car is fast, it's brutal ... it's like a 5.7 litre
vibrator.

Jeremy Clarkson on the Lamborghini Diabolo, *Motorworld*

To get a trip like this anywhere else you'd
need to sell your house and spend all the
money on acid.

Jeremy Clarkson on the Westfield S8, *The Sunday Times*

The Chrysler Stratus looks like Pamela
Anderson ... a silicone sham with no real
depth.

Jeremy Clarkson, *The Sunday Times*

Nissan QX. It exists. So does dog dirt but I
don't want any outside my house.

Jeremy Clarkson, *The Sunday Times*

To buy a Volvo 540 because it is better than
the Volvo 400 is like having someone to
dinner because they are better company than
Myra Hindley.

Jeremy Clarkson, *The Sunday Times*

As driven by all Essex aerobics instructors,
the Ann Summers Escort has all the class of a
stale Babycham.

Tiff Needell on the Ford Escort Convertible, *Top Gear*

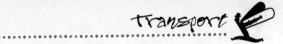

Driving this car is as enjoyable as muesli without milk.

Tiff Needell on the Austin Metro, *Top Gear*

Like a cross between a camel and a frog and about as aerodynamic as an aardvark.

Steven Greenhouse on the Deux Chevaux, *The New York Times*

The road-going equivalent of a dozen oysters.

Advertisement, Saab cars

Cars today are almost the exact equivalent of the great Gothic cathedrals; the supreme creation of an era, conceived with passion by unknown artists, and consumed in image if not in usage by a whole population which appropriates them as a purely magical object.

Roland Barthes

One enjoys the cheek of a car company that can take a panelled sitting-room, propel it down the road at over 100mph and still make as little noise as a skilled fly fisherman eating his packed lunch.

John Whiston on Rolls-Royce, *Vogue*

Anyone who can afford to buy a car more than two litres is the kind of guy who also likes to bathe in asses' milk.

Jeremy Clarkson, *Motorworld*

It's temperamental, my Fiasco, like all the best racehorses, poets and chefs.

Martin Amis, *Money*

Keep that engine purrin' like a whore on a hundred-dollar date.

John Farris, *Wildwood*

Finding a parking-space is like going to a prostitute: why pay when if you apply yourself you can get it for free?

Seinfeld, US sitcom

Politics

Politics

Politics is just like showbusiness, you have a
hell of an opening, coast for a while and
then you have a hell of a close.

Ronald Reagan

Politics ain't worrying this country
one-tenth as much as where to find a
parking-space.

Will Rogers

Government is to life what pantyhose are to
sex.

P.J. O' Rourke

If I'd lost a pound for every lie this
government told, I'd look like a bite-size
minipack of Twiglets in velour mules.

Victoria Wood

The Prime Minister is about as useful as a
catflap in an Elephant House.

Blackadder The Third

Being President is like riding a tiger. A man
has to keep on riding or be swallowed.

Harry S. Truman

Being president is like running a cemetery;
you've got a lot of people under you and
nobody's listening.

Bill Clinton

The vice-presidency is sort of like the last
cookie on the plate. Everybody insists he
won't take it, but somebody always does.

Bill Vaughan

My desire to get into Parliament was like
miners' coal dust, it was under my fingers
and I couldn't scrub it out.

Betty Boothroyd

Charles de Gaulle looked like a female llama surprised in her bath.

Winston Churchill

John Major – he makes George Bush seem like a personality.

Jackie Mason

Sir Rhodes Boyson looks like a character out of an unpublished novel by Charles Dickens.

Anon.

Like Woody Allen without the jokes.

Simon Hoggart on Sir Keith Joseph

Despite her Oxford education, her high-flying career, her media celebrity, Edwina Currie still behaves like a pushy provincial hair-saloniste queening it over her fellow passengers on a SAGA cruise to Tenerife.

Lynn Barber, *The Daily Telegraph*

I often compare Margaret Thatcher with
Florence Nightingale ... a lady with a lamp –
unfortunately, it is a blowlamp.

Denis Healey

I admire her, but it's like sitting next to
electricity.

Robert Runcie on Margaret Thatcher

It was Margaret Thatcher who first claimed
to detect similarities between William Pitt
the Younger and William Hague ... It is not a
comparison that he should encourage. Pitt,
according to Shelley, was 'stiff with everyone
but the ladies'.

Andrew Rawnsley, *The Observer*

Cecil Parkinson is *The* human equivalent of
wormwood and gall.

Jeanette Winterson

Vulcans are super-intelligent and utterly logical, resembling humans in every respect except that they have no emotions, and many have pointed ears. The new breed, like John Redwood, have their ears straightened in private clinics.

Matthew Parris, *The Times*

His reforms went down like a rat sandwich.

Dafydd Wigley on John Redwood

Tony Blair has a smile like an ageing collie.

Jan Morris

Burly and greasy-haired, John Prescott looks rather like one of those plain-talking police-men who, during the late 1970s, were always being photographed on yachting holidays with villains somewhere in the Mediterranean.

Craig Brown, *The Times*

Margaret Beckett looks like a woman resigned to walk home alone to an empty bedsit after Grab-a-Granny night at the local disco.

Richard Littlejohn, *The Sun*

He handles political crises with all the confidence of a man dialling his own telephone number.

John Bell

His argument was as thin as the homeopathic soup that was made by boiling the shadow of a pigeon that had been starved to death.

Abraham Lincoln on Stephen Douglas

We will support him as a rope supports a man who is hanged.

V.I. Lenin

I want him to kiss my ass in Macy's window at high noon and tell me it smells like roses.

Lyndon B. Johnson

 *Politics*

Like a cushion, he always bore the impress of the last man who sat on him.

David Lloyd George on Lord Derby

Making a speech on economics is a bit like pissing down your leg. It seems hot to you but never to anyone else.

Lyndon B. Johnson

Lady Veula sat listening to the speech with the stoical indifference with which an Eskimo might accept the occurrence of one snowstorm the more, in the course of an Arctic Winter.

Saki

The room erupted in spontaneous applause, very similar to what you hear at Democratic Party dinners when somebody mentions the poor.

Dave Barry, *Dave Barry's Greatest Hits*

The word 'honor' in the mouth of Mr
Webster is like the word 'love' in the mouth
of a whore.

Ralph Waldo Emerson

Like having a wardrobe fall on top of you
with the key sticking out.

Anonymous woman on having sex with Nicholas Soames,MP

For socialists, going to bed with the Liberals
is like having oral sex with a shark.

Larry Zoff

He looks like a bridegroom on a wedding
cake.

Alice Roosevelt on Thomas E. Dewey

Edward Livingstone is a man of splendid
abilities, but utterly corrupt. Like rotten
mackerel by moonlight, he shines and stinks.

John Randolph

When Lyndon Johnson wanted to persuade
you of something you really felt as if a St
Bernard had licked your face for an hour.

Benjamin C. Bradlee

Looks and sounds not unlike Hitler but
without the charm.

Gore Vidal on William F. Buckley Jr

He looks like the guy in a science fiction
movie who is first to see the Creature.

David Frye on Gerald Ford

If a tree fell in a forest and no one was there
to hear it, it might sound like Dan Quayle
looks.

Tom Shales

Boris Yeltsin is like a suitcase without a
handle: you don't really want to throw it
away but it is terribly difficult to carry.

Moscow newspaper

Law & Order

Crimes, like virtues, are their own reward.

George Farquhar

It was beautiful and simple as all truly great swindles are.

O. Henry

'Look, the police are here.'
'Yahoo, it's just like *NYPD Blue* except they have their pants on.'

Cybill, US sitcom

In England, justice is open to all – like the Ritz hotel.

James Mathew

He lies like an eye witness.

Julian Barnes

He lies like a cheap carpet.

Anon.

He uses statistics as a drunken man uses a
lamppost – for support rather than
illumination.

Andrew Lang

A cause may be inconvenient, but it's
magnificent. It's like champagne or high
shoes, and one must be prepared to suffer
for it.

Arnold Bennett

War is like love, it always finds a way.

Bertolt Brecht

We're going to go through the enemy like
crap through a goose.

George C. Scott in *Patton*, 1970

Fighting for peace is like fucking for virginity.

Anon.

Royalty

'How was your flight, your Royal Highness?'
'Have you ever flown in a plane?'
'Oh, yes, your Royal Highness, often.'
'Well, it was just like that.'

Duke of Edinburgh

Person in crowd: 'You look awfully like the
Queen.'
Queen: 'How frightfully reassuring.'

Queen Elizabeth II

If you find you are to be presented to the
Queen, do not rush up to her. She will
eventually be brought around to you, like a
dessert trolley at a good restaurant.

The Los Angeles Times

Politics

It's like live ferrets jumping around in a bag.

> Duchess of York on her bottom, *The Daily Star*

When royalty leaves the room it is like getting a seed out of your tooth.

> Mrs Paul Phipps

The Arts

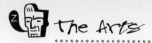

Art

I could draw like Raphael by the age of
fourteen but it took me a lifetime to draw
like a child.

Pablo Picasso

If my husband would ever meet a woman on
the street who looked like the women in his
paintings, he would fall over in a dead faint.

Mrs Pablo Picasso

Osbert had mistaken an enlarged photograph
of W.J. Turner for a map of Vesuvius.

Edith Sitwell

I do not paint a portrait to look like the
subject, rather does the person grow to look
like his portrait.

Salvador Dali

At his best Dali is like someone dressed up as Siegfried who suddenly winks at the audience in the middle of an aria.

Philip Toynbee

I couldn't have that hanging in my home. It would be like living with a gas leak.

Edith Evans on a modern painting

It makes me look as if I were straining a stool.

Winston Churchill on his portrait by Graham Sutherland

A critic told us that Damien Hirst's *A Thousand Years* – an exhibit involving maggots, a cow's head and innumerable flies being zapped on an insectocutor – was a metaphor for the human life cycle, although it seemed to me more like a metaphor for an Italian restaurant I once ate in.

Victor Lewis-Smith, *The London Evening Standard*

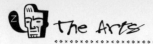

She looks as if she has just been sick or is about to be.

Noel Coward on the Mona Lisa

Henry Moore's sculptures in Hyde Park look like something that's fallen off a Jumbo Jet.

Laura Milligan

The more you look at modern art exhibits, the more everything begins to look like an exhibit, including the attendant's chair and the fire extinguisher.

Anon.

It all looks like bollocks so it must be worth something.

Jennifer Saunders on modern art, *Absolutely Fabulous*

Accusing him of hype is like rebuking a fish for being wet.

Robert Hughes on Jeff Koons

The celebrated painter Gainsborough got as much pleasure from seeing violins as from hearing them.

Georg Christoph Lichtenberg

Say, honey, you and me could make music together – and right now I feel like the L.A. Philharmonic.

Bob Hope in *My Favorite Blonde*, 1942

Music is like a dog; the nicest thing that can be said about it is that you wouldn't know it was there.

Quentin Crisp

Listening to Khatchaturian ... He called it a violin concerto. I called it a loose fan belt and the hell with it.

Raymond Chandler, *The Long Goodbye*

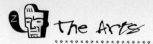 The Arts

It sounds like the kind of music a pederast
might hum when raping a choirboy.

Marcel Proust on Fauré's *Romances sans Paroles*

I like listening to Tchaikovsky's Fifth just as I
like looking at a fuchsia drenched with rain.

James Agate

Listening to the 5th Symphony of Ralph
Vaughan Williams is like staring at a cow for
45 minutes.

Aaron Copeland

I write as a sow piddles.

Wolfgang Amadeus Mozart

Some of his pages resemble a kitchen flypaper
during the rush-hour on a hot August
afternoon.

C.W. Orr on Arnold Schoenberg

❖◇×◇‹◇›◇×◇›◇×◇›◇×◇›◇×◇›◇×◇›◇×◇›◇×◇›◇×◇×◇

Beethoven always sounds to me like the
upsetting of bags of nails, with here and
there an also dropped hammer.

John Ruskin

A skeleton with pince-nez who looks as if
he's raping a 'cello.

Goncourt Brothers on Jacques Offenbach

He would dream of his piano as if it were
flesh.

Lola Haskins, *The Prodigy*

My playing is no more like hers than a lamp
is to sunshine.

Jane Austen

He dazzles the ear as a diamond does the
eye.

Anon. on Jascha Heifetz, violinist

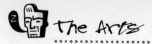 the Arts

Opera is like a husband with a foreign title: expensive to support, hard to understand, and therefore a supreme social challenge.

Cleveland Amory

The conventional prima donna's gestures: a) both hands outstretched as though pushing open a door with a heavily laden tea-tray; b) one hand suddenly raised straight on high, like Frank Chester giving Bradman out leg-before-wicket.

Neville Cardus, *The Manchester Guardian*

The acoustics in King's College Chapel would make a fart sound like a sevenfold Amen.

David Willcocks

Muzak in pubs and hotel foyers seeps round us like nerve gas.

William McIlvanney, *Surviving the Shipwreck*

⬦◇⬦◇⬦◇⬦◇⬦◇⬦◇⬦◇⬦◇⬦◇⬦◇⬦◇⬦◇⬦◇⬦◇⬦◇⬦◇⬦

Writing a musical is like doing your own
root canal work.

Don Black

A film musician is like a mortician – he can't
bring the body back to life, but he's expected
to make it look better.

Adolph Deutsch

Why is it that people in record stores act like
they're rock 'n' roll stars?'

Barry Grimmins

Singing

If white bread could sing it would sound like
Olivia Newton John.

The Sunday Telegraph Magazine

He sang like a hinge.

Ethel Merman on Cole Porter

Pavarotti is like someone who has swallowed a Stradivarius.

Peter Ustinov

Reminded me of a mezzo past her prime, straining hideously for the same note that once poured out of her throat like good vodka over ice.

Description of a trumpeter, Charlotte Carter, *Rhode Island Red*

His vibrato sounded like he was driving a tractor over ploughed fields with weights tied to his scrotum.

Spike Milligan

Bing Crosby sings like all people think they sing in the shower.

Dinah Shore

His sickly croon makes you feel like you're being force-fed caramel.

Simon Reynolds on Gary Clark, *Melody Maker*

All rock 'n' roll singers sound like a nudist backing into a cold-nosed dog —set to music.

Robert Orben

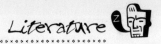

Sounds like he's pushing a wheelbarrow of wet cement up a 1 in 3 slope in a duffle coat, whining as he goes.

> Ian Gittins on singer, Fish, *Melody Maker*

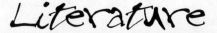

Literature

Writing is like the world's oldest profession. First you do it for your own enjoyment. Then you do it for a few friends. Eventually, you figure, 'What the hell, I might as well get paid for it.'

> Irma Kalish

The act of writing itself is done in secret, like masturbation.

> Stephen King

Don't ask a writer what he's working on. It's like asking someone with cancer about the progress of his disease.

> Anon.

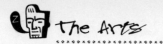

Writers. Everything has to be like something else. My head is as fluffy as whipped cream but not as sweet. More similes. I could vomit just thinking about the lousy racket.

Raymond Chandler, *The Long Goodbye*

Finishing a book is just like you took a child out in the yard and shot it.

Truman Capote

Writing a book of poetry is like dropping a rose petal down the Grand Canyon and waiting for the echo.

Don Marquis

Learning English was like moving from one darkened house to another on a starless night during a strike of candlemakers and torch-bearers.

Vladimir Nabokov

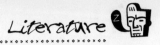
Pale Fire was alleged by Nabokov himself to be the hardest of his books to write, but that can't have compared with the pain of having to read it.

John Osborne

Correspondences are like knickers without elastic: it is impossible to keep them up.

Anon.

Nothing I have said is factual except the bits that sound like fiction.

Clive James, *Unreliable Memoires*

They're like poems, suicide notes: nearly everyone tries their hand at them some time, with or without the talent.

Martin Amis, *Money*

Ms is a syllable which sounds like a bumble bee breaking wind.

Hortense Calisher, *The New York Times*

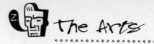

That exquisite handwriting like a fly which has been trained at the Russian ballet.

James Agate on George Bernard Shaw

Most people enjoy the sight of their own handwriting as they enjoy the smell of their own farts.

W.H. Auden

Critics are like eunuchs in a harem: they know how it's done, they've seen it done every day, but they're unable to do it themselves.

Brendan Behan

Foolish writers and readers are created for each other; and Fortune provides readers as she does mates for ugly women.

Horace Walpole

A man who has not read Homer is like a man who has not seen the ocean. There is a great object of which he has no idea.

Walter Bagehot

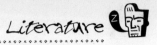
A bad experience of Shakespeare is like a
bad oyster: it puts you off for life.

Anon.

Every thought he had smelled like a rose.

T.S. Eliot on John Donne

Dr Donne's poems are like the peace of
God; they pass all understanding.

King James I

I don't like Jane Austen. She's so – so – well,
so like a tight plait.

Virginia Woolf, *The Voyage Out*

It is long and vigorous, like the penis of a
jackass.

Sydney Smith on an article by Henry Brougham

To see him fumbling with our rich and
delicate language is to experience all the
horror of seeing a Sèvres vase in the hands
of a chimpanzee.

Evelyn Waugh on Stephen Spender

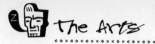 The Arts

Reading Proust is like bathing in someone else's dirty water.

Alexander Woolcott

Even when Micheál MacLíammoir took in later life to autobiographies, they were about as reliable as his hairpieces.

Sheridan Morley, *The Sunday Times*

Deems Taylor's tongue, as efficient as a buzz saw when it came to slicing fools into small pieces, was a match for Dorothy Parker's.

Marion Meade

An editor said, 'Perhaps you could just be like Dorothy Parker,' I thought, What? Keep slashing my wrists and drinking shoe polish?

Lynne Truss, *Making the Cat Laugh*

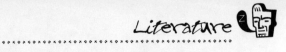

Joe Garagiola is considered something of a humorist and, like Mark Twain, is from Missouri. The resemblance is purely residential.

Jim Brosnan

Gertrude Stein and me are just like brothers.

Ernest Hemingway

Writers

He was very bald ... with the general look of an elderly fallen angel travelling incognito.

Peter Quennell on André Gide

He looked like Ramses II with his wrappings off.

Hugh Fullerton on Ring Lardner

She looked like a high altar on the move.

Elizabeth Bowen on Edith Sitwell

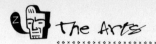 The Arts

If one is a greyhound, why try to look like a
Pekingese?

Edith Sitwell

I'm like an electric eel in a pond full of flat-
fish.

Edith Sitwell

My face looks like a wedding cake left out
in the rain.

W.H. Auden

I kept thinking, if his face looks like this,
what must his balls look like?

David Hockney on W.H.Auden's wrinkled skin as he sat for
his portrait

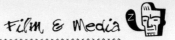

Film & Media

The media. It sounds like a convention of spiritualists.

Tom Stoppard, *Night and Day*

The events and characters depicted in this movie are fictitious. Any similarity to actual persons, living or dead, or to actual events is purely coincidental.

The film producer's disclaimer

Working for Warner Bros is like fucking a porcupine; it's a hundred pricks against one.

Wilson Mizner

Working for the Marx brothers was not unlike being chained to a galley car and lashed at ten-minute intervals.

S.J. Perelman

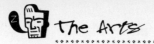
Sunday lunch at Mr Mayer's beach house was like an audience at the Vatican. Of course, it wasn't His Highness's ring you kissed.

Phil Silvers

My old films? I want to climb up there and change everything. It's like meeting a girl you slept with 15 years ago. You look at her and you think, 'My God, did I go to bed with *that*?'

Billy Wilder

Steven Spielberg returns to the underground caverns of his nightmare as obsessively as the tongue will return to the tiny cavern vacated by a loose filling.

Gilbert Adair, *The Illustrated London News*

Now Hollywood studios are just like the Ramada Inn: you rent space, you shoot and out you go.

Billy Wilder

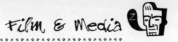
Why does the cinema feel like a treat and
the theatre, so often, like a penance?

Maureen Lipman, *Thank You For Having Me*

I find writing about the Canadian theatre of
drama depressingly like discussing the art of
dinghy-sailing among bedouins.

Merrill Denison

Television is as injurious to the soul as fast
food is to the body.

Quentin Crisp

Television, and radar and atomic energy are
so far beyond my comprehension that my
brain shudders at the thought of them and
scurries for cover like a primitive tribesman
confronted for the first time with a Dunhill
cigarette lighter.

Noel Coward

Reviewing television programmes is like
describing a road-accident to an eye-witness.

Garry Bushell

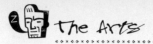
Facing the press is more difficult than
bathing a leper.

Mother Teresa

Reading someone else's newspaper is like
sleeping with someone else's wife. Nothing
seems to be precisely in the right place, and
when you find what you are looking for, it is
not clear then how to respond to it.

Malcolm Bradbury

Film & Media Reviews

About as funny as a day in bed with the
complete works of Schopenhauer.

Nigel Andrews on *Another Woman, The Financial Times*

To criticize it would be like tripping a
dwarf.

Wilfred Sheed on *Hurry Sundown, Esquire* magazine

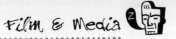

As difficult to sit through as a Black Mass
sung in Latin.

Michael Sragow on *Alien*, *The Los Angeles Herald Examiner*

As camp as a Boy Scouts' jamboree and as
corny as a chiropodists' convention.

David Aldridge on *Strictly Ballroom*, *Film Review*

As erotic as earwax.

Scheuer on *Wild Orchid*

The film goes downhill as fast as a toboggan
ride down Everest.

Christopher Tookey on *All I Want For Christmas*,
The Sunday Telegraph

The film is like the swimming-pool at a
Democratic convention, full of well-known
liberals with tiny parts: Jack Lemmon, Walter
Matthau, Ed Asner and John Candy.

Christopher Tookey on *JFK*, *The Sunday Telegraph*

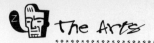
The Arts

Like watching a tea-towel dry on the radiator.

John Sessions on soap operas

It looks like pornography without the sex.

Anon. on *Eldorado*

Getting the costumes right in *The Cleopatras* was like polishing the fish knives on the *Titanic*.

Julian Barnes

As grisly as an undertaker's picnic and maybe grislier.

Robert Cushman on *The Little Foxes*

That was a truly awful night in the theatre. I walked out feeling like Mrs Lincoln.

Cybill, US sitcom

Celebrities

A celebrity is any well-known TV or movie star who looks like he spends more than two hours working with his hair.

Steve Martin

Breasts like granite and a brain like Swiss cheese, full of holes.

Billy Wilder on Marilyn Monroe

She was good at playing abstract confusion in the same way that a midget is good at being short.

Clive James on Marilyn Monroe

As wholesome as a bowl of cornflakes and at least as sexy.

Dwight Macdonald on Doris Day

More of a mystery than cot death.

Rex Reed on the career of Sylvester Stallone

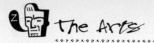 the Arts

Like a brown condom full of walnuts.

Clive James on Arnold Schwarzenegger's physique.

I have had myself rebuilt. I'm the female
equivalent of a counterfeit $20 bill.

Cher

Alfred Hitchcock thought of himself as
looking like Cary Grant. That's tough, to
think of yourself one way and look another.

Tippi Hedren

His face had that look people get when they
ride in elevators.

Anatole Broyard on Steve McQueen

The man's ears make him look like a taxicab
with both doors open.

Howard Hughes on Clark Gable

Oh, for the gift of Rostand's *Cyrano* to evoke
the vastness of that nose alone as it cleaves
the giant screen from east to west, bisects it
from north to south. It zigzags across our
horizon like a bolt of fleshy lightning; it
towers like a ziggurat made of meat.

John Simon on Barbra Streisand, *New York*

Howard Hughes said one time: 'My God,
Mitch, you're just like a pay toilet — you
don't give a shit for nothin'.'

Robert Mitchum

A parrot around Tallulah must feel as
frustrated as a kleptomaniac in a piano store.

Fred Allen on Tallulah Bankhead

A day away from Tallulah is like a month in
the country.

Howard Dietz on Tallulah Bankhead

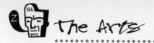

Pola Negri had a blind and uncritical admiration of her own genius in the blaze of which her sense of humour evaporated like a dew-drop on a million-watt arc lamp.

Rodney Ackland

He had a face, even in his 20s, which looked as though he had rented it on a long lease and had lived in it so long he didn't want to move out.

David Niven on George Sanders

He looks like an extra from a crowd scene by Hieronymus Bosch.

Kenneth Tynan on Don Rickles

As usual he looked just like Joan of Arc – after she's burnt at the stake.

Anon. on John Hurt

I'm not as normal as I appear.

Woody Allen

Peter Bogdanovich is *weird*, and like all the most seriously weird people he looks perfectly ordinary.

Lynn Barber, *The Independent on Sunday*

Charlotte Rampling always sounds to me like an active verb.

Bernard Levin

The sloppy sweater with long sleeves is a Julia Roberts speciality that allows her to dangle her arms and act like Bambi getting lost in the forest. I have tried this in front of the mirror and, believe me, you need talent to pull it off.

Anne Billson, *The New Statesman*

Noel Coward invented the concept of cool. And if his face suggested an old boot, it was unquestionably hand-made.

Kenneth Tynan

I was photographed ... on one occasion sitting up in an over-elaborate bed looking like a heavily-doped Chinese illusionist.

Noel Coward

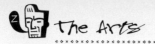

To me, Edith looks like something that would eat its young.

> Dorothy Parker on Edith Evans

Edith Evans took her curtain calls as though she had just been un-nailed from the cross.

> Noel Coward

Billie Whitelaw plays Josephine with the effortless desperation of Rubinstein playing 'Chopsticks'.

> Clive James

An ego like a raging tooth.

> W.B. Yeats on Mrs Patrick Campbell

Like a Goth swaggering around Rome wearing an onyx toilet seat for a collar, he exudes self-confidence.

> Clive James on Rupert Murdoch

He looked rather like a Catholic priest on his night off.

> Quentin Crisp on Divine

I'd feel ugly if I wasn't decked out like a drag queen's Christmas tree.

Dolly Parton

Michael Jackson looks like a Barbie doll that has been whittled by a malicious brother.

Thomas Sutcliffe, *The Independent*

I've always looked like a bank clerk who freaked out.

Elton John

Like a stoat on amphetamines ... she makes Dame Edna seem low-key.

Lynn Barber on Barbara Cartland, *The Daily Telegraph*

Twin miracles of mascara, her eyes looked like the corpses of two small crows that had crashed into a chalk cliff.

Clive James on Barbara Cartland

Barbara Cartland ... with false eyelashes, as thick as those caterpillars that give you a rash if you handle them.

Alan Clark, *Diaries*

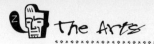

He looks rather like King Edward – the potato not the monarch.

Anon. on Ian Hislop

Loyd Grossman's impersonation of an American intellectual was always about as plausible as Douglas Bader captaining the British synchronized swimming team.

Victor Lewis-Smith, *The London Evening Standard*

As earthy and wide open as the North Texas spaces she hails from.

Playboy on Anna Nicole Smith

Ms Anthea Turner had all the allure of a glacé cherry, together with a hairstyle reminiscent of a marmoset or one of those furry creatures which bob in the back of cars.

Harry Eyres, *The Spectator*

Brian Redhead looks like every Morris dancer you have ever seen.

Stephen Pile

'I have twenty thousand books,' Jeremy Beadle boasted, which is rather like learning that Stephen Hawking has twenty thousand pairs of trainers.

Victor Lewis-Smith, *The London Evening Standard*

A woman with a heavily lived-in face poised unceremoniously on top of a torso like a dressmaker's dummy.

Paul Johnson on Lynn Barber, *The Spectator*

Why is Melvyn Bragg somehow sacred, like the Queen Mother?

Lynn Barber, *The Independent*

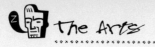

Index

Index

Index

Index

Index

◇◆◇

Index

Index

Index

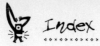

Index

Text Acknowledgments

The publishers and author are grateful to the following for permission to publish extracts from copyright material

Other People © Martin Amis 1981, *Money* © Martin Amis 1984, *London Fields* © Martin Amis 1989 by permission of Jonathan Cape, a division of Random House UK Ltd; *The Information* © Martin Amis 1995 by permission of Flamingo, a division of HarperCollins Publishers; *Dave Barry's Greatest Hits* © Dave Barry 1988 by permission of Pan Books, a division of Macmillan Publishers Ltd; *Dave Barry's Complete Guide to Guys* © Dave Barry 1995 by permission of Warner Books, a division of Little, Brown and Company (UK); excerpt from *The Abortion* by Richard Brautigan. Copyright © 1970, 1971 by Richard Brautigan. Reprinted by permission of Houghton Miffin Company. All rights reserved. *Dreaming of Babylon* © Richard Brautigan 1977, *Revenge of the Lawn* © Richard Brautigan by permission of Ianthe Brautigan; *Trout Fishing in America* © Richard Brautigan 1967; *Willard and his Bowling Trophies: A Perverse Mystery* © Richard Brautigan 1976 by permission of Jonathan Cape, a division of Random House UK Ltd; *Rhode Island Red* © Charlotte Carter, 1997 reprinted by kind permission of Serpent's Tail, London; excerpts from works by Raymond Chandler © The Estate of Raymond Chandler by permission of Penguin Books; *Four Weddings and a Funeral* © Richard Curtis 1994. Reprinted by permission of the Peters Fraser and Dunlop Group Limited on behalf of Richard Curtis and Polygram Film Production GmbH; *Collected Poems* 1901–1962 © T.S. Eliot 1963 by permission of Faber and Faber Ltd; *The Kinky Friedman Crime Club* © Kinky Friedman 1986, 1987, 1988, 1992, *More Kinky Friedman* © Kinky Friedman 1989, 1991, 1993, *God Bless John Wayne* © Kinky Friedman 1995 by permission of Faber and Faber Ltd; *Jeremy Hardy Speaks to the Nation* © Jeremy Hardy © Kathy Lette 1993 by permission of Picador, a division of Macmillan Publishers Ltd; *Inside the Magic Rectangle* © Victor Lewis-Smith 1995 by permission of Victor Gollancz Ltd, a division of Cassell plc; *Remedy is None* © William McIlvanney 1966, *Laidlaw* © William McIlvanney 1977, *The Papers of Tony Veitch* © William McIlvanney 1983, *The Big Man* © William McIlvanney 1985,